PLATEAU JUMPING

Jeremy -
I don't expect you to read
all of this but since you
are featured on p. 64 I
wanted you to have a copy.
You inspired me!
Thanks
Shaun

PLATEAU JUMPING

WHAT to Change When **CHANGE** Is What You **WANT**

SHAWN D. SMITH

Niche Pressworks
Indianapolis, IN

PLATEAU JUMPING

Copyright © 2024 by SHAWN D. SMITH

All rights reserved. No part of this book may be used or reproduced in any manner whatsoever without prior written consent of the author, except as provided by the United States of America copyright law.

The content provided in this book is for informational purposes only. It does not constitute financial, investment, or tax advice. The information shared herein should not be taken as personalized advice or recommendations. Readers are encouraged to consult with a qualified financial or tax professional before making any decisions based on the content of this book. Any stories or anecdotes about clients included in this book are based on real experiences; however, names and certain identifying details have been changed or consolidated to protect confidentiality and ensure privacy. No story directly corresponds to a single, identifiable individual.
In addition, while every effort has been made to accurately represent stories and accounts involving other individuals, some details may have been altered, paraphrased, or interpreted to fit the context. Any inaccuracies or misrepresentations are unintentional.

For permission to reprint portions of this content or bulk purchases, contact shawn@decidedlypodcast.com

Published by Niche Pressworks; NichePressworks.com
Indianapolis, IN

ISBN
Hardcover: 978-1-962956-04-8
Paperback: 978-1-962956-11-6
eBook: 978-1-962956-05-5

The views expressed herein are solely those of the author and do not necessarily reflect the views of the publisher.

For my son Sanger.

Without your encouragement, these thoughts and ideas would have never reached the next plateau.

Table of Contents

INTRODUCTION

A Long-Awaited Journey

"Sometimes it's the journey that teaches you a lot about your destination."
— DRAKE, CANADIAN RAPPER

"The real voyage of discovery consists not in seeking new landscapes, but in having new eyes." — MARCEL PROUST, NOVELIST

I STOOD AT the black granite conference table in my fourth-floor office, wearing my hiking boots. My overstuffed backpack leaned against the wall behind me as I put my signature on the next document and the one after that.

I was signing the papers to sell my wealth management business. All the client files, art, furniture, and equipment — everything I had built over thirty years except a few long-term client relationships — would be sold. Soon, I would be working for the new owners to provide coaching and maintain those few long-term client relationships. For how long, I didn't know.

Finally, I reached the last signature. Now free, I stepped back, grabbed my pack, and unceremoniously walked out.

Then I kept walking.

LEAVING A LEGACY OF MORE THAN MONEY AND THINGS

I had started thinking about the sale eighteen months earlier while working with two of my clients, Dave and Pamela.

They had been married for forty years. Dave had been tinkering with the idea of retirement for the past five, though without enthusiasm. We had run the numbers over and over, but he never was able to find that special something to retire to. It always seemed like he was just leaving work with no better plan.

Finally, I said uncharacteristically bluntly, "Dave, you've got all the money you both will ever need. Find something that excites you, and do that. If you don't want to work any longer, then don't. If you like working, do that, but you've got to decide what you want to occupy your time and find the purpose that pulls you toward it. You can't keep not deciding." Embarrassingly, my suggestion came more out of frustration at his indecision than out of the empathy I should have had.

Three months after our discussion, Dave retired. Six months after his retirement, Pamela fell from her car on her way into church. She was rushed to the ICU and never left.

At the funeral, Dave pulled me aside. "Shawn, I don't think I would have retired if you hadn't encouraged me. If I hadn't retired, I would have missed the last six months with Pam. It wasn't enough. This sure wasn't what we planned. But I wouldn't have had that time with her at all if I hadn't left work when I did. What was important was being there with her these last six months." His eyes glassy, he put his hand on my shoulder and thanked me.

I felt I didn't deserve the thanks, but before I could respond, someone else broke in to offer more condolences.

Then, the moment was gone, and I drifted to the outer edge of the circle of mourners.

Within a year, Dave also passed away. He was only 62.

When his three daughters came to my office to close out the estate, I shared what Dave had told me about his final six months with their mom.

They were all set to receive an inheritance that would change their lives. But Dave left more than money. He left a realization with all of us that life was finite and that figuring out what you want and making it happen take careful decision-making and action. He left his daughters the knowledge that they should seek something meaningful and pull close those relationships that matter.

Confronted with Dave and Pamela's situation, I realized I needed to do some deep thinking of my own. What was next for me?

Tough Decisions Lead to New Growth

My next meeting with my business coach, Chuck, was a good time to start talking about what I wanted to do next.

"I'm thinking about selling my practice," I blurted out. May as well jump right into the subject before I could hesitate.

This wasn't a light decision. I had directed more than thirty years' worth of time and energy toward this business. But now, I wanted to scale back and change what I was doing. What happened to Dave and Pam had impacted me. There were things I had always wanted or needed to do yet never had done — things I would regret never doing.

I wanted more time with my wife and family, who had been neglected over the years of late nights at the office. I wanted more meaningful relationships with friends. I wanted growth in a different and meaningful way.

"Now that you know this, you can't unknow it," Chuck said.

He was right. The thoughts of selling my practice began to affect my decisions. I couldn't put it out of my mind.

That's why, a year and a half later, I finally made the sale. Without missing a beat, I began the next phase of my life's journey — hiking the Pacific Crest Trail, starting at the US-Mexico border. From there, the trail led all the way north to Canada. I wasn't certain how far I'd go, but I was certain I was leaving behind the feeling of stagnation — and that I would learn something important. There is something about unplugging and walking through nature that will teach you things if you'll let it.

This book is the culmination of those lessons. It is about what came next.

I started noticing that the way things happen along the trail was eerily similar to the way life works. What I learned about how to navigate the trail could also apply to navigating the different landscapes of life. Sure, they are metaphorical landscapes, but the metaphor works. I'll tell you about some of what I learned in the pages following, but for now, let's just say it changed my life. I had a fresh perspective — a new way of seeing things.

However, it didn't answer all my questions. In fact, when I returned to Texas and to the small group of clients I had retained after the sale, I found my questions had only become deeper. Suddenly, I realized what I *didn't* know.

This realization made me change my entire approach to my business.

I started thinking, what if I stopped asking clients what goals they wanted to achieve and started asking *why* they wanted to achieve them?

I wanted to stop assuming someone's money was important to them and start asking *why* it was important to them. I wanted to stop responding to questions with quick answers and advice and start asking clients to tell me more about what genuine advice they were seeking. Not every decision they sought to make was a financial or mathematical one. Sometimes, they were deeper. I planned on asking different and better questions to find out which. By doing that, I could make a much greater impact in others' lives for the better.

That was how my own life changed. Now, what about yours?

My hope is that through these pages, I can start you on your own journey, whatever that looks like for you. Through showing you glimpses of what I learned along the trail, I hope to give you some ideas you can apply in your own life. It's always good to have a trail guide who's familiar with the landscape. I may not know everything about dealing with change, but what I do know, I'm willing to share. If you're ready to take your own first step, read on.

SECTION 1

LISTENING AND LEARNING: Lessons from the Trail

The Pacific Crest Trail stretches from the US-Mexico border all the way north to Canada. Starting at the southern border, one traverses a rich, diverse desert landscape. Sometimes, you're climbing up. Other times, the ground levels out to a plateau, giving you time to rest. There's always another canyon wall around the next corner, and to move further, you have to climb up or down, higher or lower. What you find along the way is rarely what you expect. But one thing is certain: No matter where you find yourself, the journey is never dull.

CHAPTER 1

Moving Through the Plateaus

CHANGE JUMPS STAGNATION

"Sometimes the questions are complicated, and the answers are simple."
— DR. SEUSS

"What you see and what you hear depends a great deal on where you are standing. It also depends on what sort of person you are." — C.S. LEWIS

"Without change there is no innovation, creativity, or incentive for improvement. Those who initiate change will have a better opportunity to manage the change that is inevitable." — WILLIAM POLLARD

AS I HIKED along the Pacific Crest Trail (PCT), the lessons came quickly. The first one was particularly noteworthy.

It happened a little more than a week after I started my trip. I was hiking through the snow one morning when I began to sense something was off. Few hikers moved though this early in the season. Snow still covered the trail at high elevations, and with the trail completely hidden beneath the blanket of white, navigation was a challenge.

I noticed footprints in the snow and began to follow along, assuming this was the trail. Placing my steps inside the other person's tracks, one after the other, made walking easier. In this manner, I hiked all morning up Mount San Jacinto in Southern California.

When I stopped and looked at the map to check my progress along the PCT, I realized I was off course — not only no longer on the trail but nowhere near it. Following in these footsteps had made things easier, but it turned out I was moving away from where I wanted to be.

I didn't want to admit I was lost. Yet I couldn't seem to get back on track, either. It seemed everywhere I turned took me to a new place I didn't want to be. I wasn't just lost — I was also mentally stuck and unsure where to turn.

I realized I had been mindlessly just going in a direction out of inertia but not thinking about my destination.

Hoping for a shortcut, I began to make my way down to where I believed I would rejoin the trail. As I descended, I could hear a noise down below. To my inexperienced ears, it sounded like a roadway with cars moving by. However, as I approached, I realized it was a rapidly flowing stream. With snowfall over sixty percent higher than normal this year, the streams were larger than I had expected.

The problem was that I needed to be on the other side of this one.

I searched up and down for a place to cross. Not finding any, I made my way through the thick brush upstream. The branches of the underbrush grabbed at my pack and pulled at me as if to tell me to stop.

I found a place where a large pine tree had fallen across the stream. Carefully making my way through the brush,

I headed over to step onto the tree, which would be my bridge. I inched my way across, now standing a good ten feet above the roaring waters below me as they churned over the smooth, round boulders. Boulders that, I suddenly realized, would end this journey if I crashed down onto them.

As I crept across, something shifted — either the tree or, more likely, my wobbly knees. In that split second, I didn't know which.

"Shit!" I shouted for no one to hear as I jammed my hiking pole into the tree for balance.

My heart thumped in my chest, and a thought leapt into my mind. *If I fall from here, there will be a local story of some guy who got lost in the woods and was never found.* That story would be me. No one knew exactly where I was. I wasn't on the trail. I wasn't where a sane person would be. I was unfindable.

"There must be a better way to get where I need to be," I said to myself. I squatted down and straddled the tree, very slowly backing off, inch by inch, sliding along as my hiking poles dangled above the roaring stream. Carefully, I approached the bank. With a caution inspired by visions of slipping in from the steep, sloping bank at the last second, I firmly stepped back to the ledge, grabbed a small sapling, and pulled myself up and onto the safety of the snowy bank.

"That was stupid," I muttered.

But we do stupid things when we're stuck. When we feel trapped, our decision-making quality falls off the map. I was using this experience to get unstuck, but I found myself getting stuck anyway.

Retracing my steps back away from the stream, I noted my first set of lessons.

Know where you are.

Know where you're going.

Know when you're stuck,
and find a better way forward.

Thankful now for the footprints in the snow, I found my way back to the mystery person's tracks and retraced my steps back the way I had come.

I finally found the five-foot-tall trail sign I had missed earlier. It was easy to miss, barely peeking up from beneath the several feet of snow I stood upon.

Why was I following in others' footsteps when I didn't know where they were leading? They obviously weren't going where I was going. Either that, or they were as lost as I was.

It's easy to get off course when the path isn't clear. The problem occurs when we are in the wrong place, heading in the wrong direction, or, in some cases, moving along the trail for all the wrong reasons or motivations. The problems occur when the true seeking stops.

I noted more lessons.

Don't follow people when you
don't know where they're going.

Look carefully for hidden signs.

The path forward becomes unclear when you're lost.

This list was quickly getting longer.

Back on track, I became more aware and noticed more. I noticed how the trail moved. I noticed how the terrain repeated but was new at the same time.

For three months and more than a thousand miles, the trail became my mentor. As I ascended to new heights, I noticed the transitions in the landscape and how they matched up to the transitions I saw in my life. Through the ups and downs, I noticed that the plateaus I reached were places of rest and reflection, where I could see more clearly and chart a course forward. Every new valley had its own character. Every new hilltop had its own lessons. Speaking of which... I'd learned another lesson.

Take time to notice what you see when you plateau.

Resting up on a hillside one morning, I noticed a small group of hikers on the trail below me. They were heading up in my direction. The climb ahead was going to be brutal. I quickly grabbed my pack and continued up. I'm competitive, and I wasn't going to let them catch me, but I was struggling.

I glanced back and saw they had gained on me. I quickened my pace. As the trail turned along the ridge of the mountain, I noticed that they were advancing quickly. I sped up even more.

Now, I was almost jogging up the mountain. Finally, I heard them behind me. I stepped off the trail to let them pass.

"Good morning!" they said, smiling and waving as they approached. We traded the normal questions and answers: "When did you start on the PCT? How far are you going?" And then, as quickly as they arrived, they were off, hiking at a pace that would have exhausted a mountain goat. Soon, they were gone.

FOR THREE MONTHS

AND MORE THAN

A THOUSAND MILES,

THE TRAIL BECAME

MY MENTOR.

I realized I was competing with hikers who didn't know they were competing with me. Why was I trying to outpace these hikers? I looked within to my own competitiveness and motivations and didn't like what I saw. Another lesson.

Hike your own hike.

I slowed my pace and took in the beauty around me. I didn't need to rush this.

I also didn't need to avoid or get out of the plateaus I reached. Instead, I could use them to stop and learn.

As I paused to reflect, I noticed things.

I realized that, although I longed for breaks, once I got to a plateau where I could stop, I still wanted to keep going.

I noticed how I struggled at certain parts.

I noticed what questions I needed to ask. Most often, I asked myself, "Where, exactly, am I? Am I still heading in the right direction? What do I think the trail ahead holds for me?" I would check the topography in advance, determining the elevation changes and how to get to the next stopping point. I would make sure I had enough fresh water and food.

Check progress and direction frequently.

The endless plateaus, or pauses, were teaching me something, and I began to look forward to them.

At the thousand-mile mark, the snow and the swollen streams were getting worse. The snow was making some areas impassable. At least to me. As a solo hiker, I still had the voice in my head, screaming at me to be careful at every stream crossing. It was at that marker that I realized something.

I think I've received what I came for.

That realization made my decision. The trail had given me enough teaching for now. After a thousand miles, I was ready to head home and put my lessons to work, not only for myself but for others, too.

DISCOVER WHAT IS IMPORTANT

My first meeting upon returning to the office after being gone for three months was with long-time clients Nancy and Harry. Harry was a quiet man, twenty years his wife's senior. Nancy was a no-nonsense woman who had retired as an account executive from a Fortune 500 company three years prior.

After Nancy's retirement, she and Harry had throttled back their lifestyle — all the way back.

We sat down at that same black granite conference table on which I had signed away most of my business three months before. Nancy and Harry were two of my few remaining clients. We chatted about our lives for a couple of minutes. They asked about my PCT hike, and we caught up on how their grandkids were doing.

We'd met like this many other times. But with the lessons from my trip fresh in my mind, I planned to handle today's meeting differently. All the normally reviewed investment reports and performance statements sat in a closed folder on the table, ready to be brought out if this didn't go well or I chickened out — it was up to me.

I didn't hesitate. Instead, I started asking probing questions.

"We have been dealing with your investments for years," I said. "This money is obviously important to you. What I need to ask you is, *what* is important about this money to you?"

Silence. Then Nancy spoke. "Well, we don't want to lose it!"

They laughed. But I persisted.

"Right, but what's important about not losing it?"

They stopped laughing. "What do you mean?"

"Obviously, you don't want to lose your money. But... what's important about not losing it?"

"It's our security," Nancy answered.

"Tell me more about that."

"I don't want to worry about running out," she said. "I want to know if I'm going to be ok so we can go spend money and do things together and help our grandkids if they need it." She paused and took a breath. "We live our lives in fear right now. You know, sort of stuck. Concerns about money hold us back. I want to feel secure so we can have the freedom mentally to do what we always talk about doing. We talk about them, but then we don't do them." In silent agreement, Harry took her hand, and Nancy smiled briefly as her eyes got a slight bit watery.

I was determined to dig until we had uncovered what was really at their core. I started taking notes. We were really beginning to locate where they were on their plateau. "Those things you want to do. What would they look like?" I knew visualizing the next plateau would help.

Harry, who had been silent, chimed in for the first time. "We have always wanted to go to New Zealand. But it's so expensive," he said in his slow, deliberate way. Nancy glanced away, and I could tell there was more to that story.

But then she changed the subject. "I've wanted to do volunteer work and to take some classes. Maybe photography."

They kept sharing, and our meeting ran longer than any of our previous ones as they got energized about the future.

Nancy and Harry were on a plateau. We spent our meeting locating where they were in relation to where they wanted to be and deciding what actions they needed to take to jump to their new destination.

In the past, I would have just tried to elicit a financial goal from someone. Later, I would have wondered why they never took the trip, started volunteering, or bought the boat or second home as they'd said they wanted to do.

I realized I had been looking at it wrong. Travels to exotic places and photography classes weren't the goals. They were just the markers that would tell them they were moving to a place of mental security and freedom from worry. That was the real objective: to live without worry. The larger vision was to feel secure so they could put their wealth to a greater purpose. Deep down, they wanted to be charitable to their community and help their grandchildren. Worry held them back.

Nancy and Harry had never felt ready to jump to the next plateau because they had never dealt with their emotional state on the current plateau. They hadn't connected their next plateau to what was truly important and placed goals in the right perspective. They hadn't figured out what levers to pull to move forward.

WHY WE NEED PLATEAUS: A FRESH PERSPECTIVE

The typical view of plateaus as a negative place where existence is mired in eternal stagnation is plain wrong. The plateau isn't a place you stay but part of a continuum. It's just a pause before you move on.

When you are learning and growing, short plateau periods can be beneficial. A study conducted in 2019 investigated the effects of plateauing on learning and performance in a computer-based game.[1] The researchers recruited participants to play a computer game in which they navigated a maze to find hidden objects. The participants were randomly assigned to one of three groups. The first group played the game with a gradually increasing level of difficulty. The second group played with a fixed level of difficulty. Finally, a third group played with a gradually decreasing level of difficulty.

Interestingly, the results showed that the second group, which played with a fixed level of difficulty (i.e., plateaued), demonstrated better retention of knowledge and skills, higher levels of motivation, and better game performance compared to the other groups.

Not only are you divinely created to spend time on a plateau learning, reflecting, and growing from the experience, but it's a good thing that you do. The plateau should be meditated upon and cherished. It provides opportunities for rejuvenation, reflection, growth, and learning.

A Plateau Brings Stability

One advantage of plateauing is that, after striving for growth and advancement, reaching a plateau provides security and reduces stress and uncertainty. It allows you to savor your achievements, enjoy the fruits of your labor, and find solace in the present moment.

Far from being inescapable periods of stagnation, plateaus can, in fact, offer opportunities for growth and development.

In fact, much of what others say about plateaus gives the wrong perspective. Think about a plateau as an upside-down bowl on top of which you are sitting like a small marble. You can try to stay comfortably balanced on top, but you are more likely to roll off one direction or the other. Where you roll is up to you. The more you know about how to navigate the landscape, the better your decisions will be.

So, for example, if you are on a weight-loss or physical training journey and what you've been doing slowly stops working, you're on a plateau. Great! Now you know something. You know that what used to work now needs to change. You also know if you just do what you've been doing, you won't arrive where you want to be. Worse, if you revert to doing what you used to do before your weight-loss journey began, you'll end up in a place you never wanted to be.

Plateaus are not a place of permanence where you get intractably stuck. You don't level off or roll to the bottom of a plateau and become unable to climb out. You roll off a plateau because you can't stay there. You know you are reluctant to let go of where you are, but at the same time, you know you can't hold on, either. You don't want to slip back, but neither do you want to stand still. And so, you jump.

Embrace Change

If change is inevitable, why not embrace it?

You *will* move through the plateaus. You will experience different stress levels, emotions, energy consumption, and challenges as well as benefits.

The second law of thermodynamics states that matter moves from a state of order to disorder. That's entropy. Entropy acts on everything, including you. Without care and attention, it's easy to get out of alignment with what you envision for yourself and the current plateau you inhabit. There will be that reckoning when you realize that your real self, as defined by your *actions*, isn't matching up with your image of yourself, defined by your *thoughts*.

To paraphrase the Greek philosopher Heraclitus, the only certainty in life is change. When moving with the changes, you need to look to how you can best grow so as to avoid simply leaving where you are. Your new place should ideally be more aligned with your true motivations, values, and purpose.

You've seen it before: Someone retires from their job but has no compelling new purpose calling them. Without a bigger, better future waiting for them, they find the next plateau lacking. Soon, travel and golf lose their luster, and they find themselves searching for a new purpose.

Your time on the plateau is a continual effort to constrain entropy to your desired limits. But eventually, you must make your way to the next plateau. The secret is to embrace that reality and stay adaptable. Nancy and Harry didn't need the landscape to change — they needed to change their beliefs about the landscape and increase their understanding of their goals and how to achieve them. They needed to connect through relationships to make meaningful differences in the lives of others. In this way, they could feel more secure in making their next jump.

THE REAL CHALLENGE: MOVEMENT WITH PURPOSE

The plateau's real challenge is not that you will get permanently stuck there but that you may move from it to a place you don't want to go when you aren't ready to move. By seeing change as an opportunity for growth, you'll find yourself enjoying it more. One way to think of it is as controlled evolution, with you being the one in control.

The idea of plateaus in evolution has been around since the 1970s, when paleontologists Niles Eldredge and Stephen Jay Gould put forth their theory of "punctuated equilibrium" as an alternative to the then-prevailing view that evolution occurs gradually, evenly, and continuously over extended periods of time. Instead, punctuated equilibrium theorized that species experience prolonged periods of relative stability or stasis, interrupted by brief periods of rapid evolutionary change or speciation events.[2]

These bursts of change are often associated with environmental pressures, such as changes in climate or the introduction of new predators or competitors. The theory suggests that these bursts of change result in the formation of new species, which then enter a period of stasis until the next burst of change occurs.

An interesting sociology study back in 1964 seems to support the punctuated equilibrium concept. The study examined the work habits of engineers in a large manufacturing company. It found that the engineers spent most of their time engaged in routine work with the attending strain and coping requirements that come along with it. These periods of work were then separated by short pauses (or breaks) with occasional bursts of innovation and creativity, after which they would jump to a new level of performance. In other words, the routine "plateaus" enabled the performance jumps.[3]

A Clear Path Will Take You Further

So, how can you take control of change in your life? The best way is to have a sense of purpose and realize that there will be plateaus; your purpose will evolve over time.

Like Nancy and Harry, many people set short-term goals without a sense of what they really want. They may achieve these goals, but they won't feel satisfied. The reason is simple: They're following someone else's footprints in the snow, taking an unknown path, unsure where they are heading and getting off track from where they truly want to be. They're doing what others are doing or telling them to do. They don't know what they themselves really want or what's holding them back from getting it.

In Nancy's and Harry's case, beliefs held them back. To deal with that, we visualized what a change in beliefs would look like and how it would help them find a new way to approach their relationship to their own wealth and each other.

We looked at their situation through this new lens of purpose and security. Their goals of volunteering and helping the grandkids showed they wanted to have influence in other's lives. Nancy's vision of a larger purpose led her to begin volunteering at a local mission. She and Harry started taking care of the grandkids a couple of days a week, working to build a stronger relationship with them and each other. With their new vision, Nancy and Harry were moving to their next plateau.

A few months later, Nancy and Harry flew to New Zealand. Nancy was still volunteering at a local mission, and we had set up a charitable foundation in their name. Their foundation would support Nancy's work at the local mission.

They now realized they had been on a plateau that had stopped satisfying them. But by envisioning what they wanted to change and aligning it with their motivations, they were able to take action to move somewhere better. By aligning their purpose and actions, they jumped.

NAVIGATING THE LANDSCAPE OF LIFE

On my hike, I noticed something important: Plateaus don't always need to be higher. They don't need to be more. They just need to be directionally aligned with your larger purpose. They should be what you need at the time.

They need to be right.

This momentary pause of the plateau can allow space for reflection. In our relentless pursuit of future goals and milestones, we often overlook the significance of the journey itself.

Stepping back from the constant treadmill of progress allows you to gain perspective and refocus your efforts on what truly matters. It is a time for self-inventory and self-awareness, enabling you to evaluate desires, goals, and aspirations. It's a time to determine why you want to change.

Now that we've looked at the importance of plateaus, we'll take a look at how change can happen by exploring the different phases of the plateau landscape.

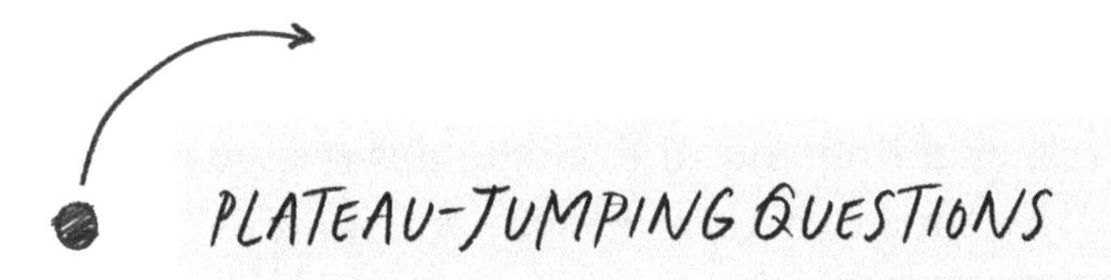

In what areas of life am I on a plateau?

What advantages or opportunities exist on my current plateau?

What fears do I have about leaving the current plateau?

CHAPTER 2

Navigating the Phases

KNOWLEDGE JUMPS THE UNKNOWN

"Success is not final, failure is not fatal: It is the courage to continue that counts." —WINSTON CHURCHILL

"Don't be afraid to give up the good to go for the great." —JOHN D. ROCKEFELLER

"Life begins at the end of your comfort zone." —NEALE DONALD WALSCh

SOMETIMES, YOU NEED to get away from where you are comfortable to realize that what you know to be true about yourself really isn't.

I didn't know this yet as I gazed out the dusty truck window to the bleak desert landscape rolling by. For the moment, I was just a dad on a road trip with his daughter.

My daughter Summer and I, along with my cousin Will and two Tibetan guides, were traveling across the vast Tibetan Plateau. It's the largest plateau in the world. Known as the "roof of the world," it sits at an average elevation of 14,800 feet and covers 970,000 square miles. That's higher than any point in the Rocky Mountains and larger than the state of Alaska.[4]

We had left Lhasa (the former home of the Dalai Lama) the previous day and were still another day's drive from where we would start our hike. As the endless rocky hills passed by, unchanging for hours, I had time to reflect. Lhasa was at an elevation of nearly 12,000 feet. Now, we were ascending even higher, but too slowly for my liking.

Once we left the plateau, we would gain in elevation quickly and then hike up even higher. We would hike to the base camp of what our guide called Mount Chomolungma, or as I had always known it, Mount Everest. All I could think about was getting off the Tibetan Plateau and finally being at the base camp I had envisioned for so long.

We finally got to the literal end of the road, shouldered our backpacks, and started our hike. I soon realized that whatever physical preparation I thought I had made was not enough. I now wished I had done more. Living in the flat lowlands of Texas had not prepared me for the thinning air.

As we quickly approached the 17,000-foot elevation where base camp waited, hiking became more difficult. Breathing became harder, and my appetite all but disappeared. Altitude sickness was setting in. I had ascended too quickly and arrived at a place I wasn't ready for.

We finally arrived. Exhausted, we slowly set up our flimsy nylon tents. They provided a respite from the brutal wind but not from the incessant noise of the wind battering their sides. All I wanted to do was rest, but for now, that seemed impossible. My head was throbbing.

I got out of the tent and started walking around the rocky terrain, hoping that would help.

I had dreamed for years of being at the base camp of Everest. I had envisioned looking back down across the Himalayas and then looking up another 12,000 feet to Everest's summit.

In a few months, climbing season would come, and this area would transform. Others more ambitious than I would try to ascend to that summit. They would arrive here and experience a different base camp — one bustling with climbers, guides, and support personnel.

Today, it was vacant.

I was alone with my thoughts. A hundred feet below, Summer and Will sat outside our tents. The Tibetan guides had opted to stay at a camp even lower in elevation, with more comforts.

I sat and watched as the clouds moved on an endless loop, briefly revealing and then hiding the summit.

I always believed I could climb anything. Higher places were always attainable. But now, reality settled in as with labored breathing, I contemplated the impact of my comfortable lifestyle on my physical ability. My lungs were laughing at me and my goal of climbing a mountain like this.

I was at a high point geographically and a low point mentally.

It seems that although you may try, you're never fully able to envision the climb until you're there. Living it. Doing it. The vision leaves out the realities of what we experience once we're there.

My vision of how this hike would go left out the fact that the area where we hiked was higher than any point I had previously climbed. It had left out how exactly I should ascend to that level to avoid altitude sickness. I had moved too quickly, and now I was paying the price.

IT SEEMS THAT
ALTHOUGH YOU MAY
TRY, YOU'RE NEVER
FULLY ABLE TO
ENVISION THE CLIMB
UNTIL YOU'RE THERE.

As I sat thinking, I noticed something interesting and unexpected about this place: There were fossils of sea creatures up here on this mountain.

Encased in rock now sitting miles above sea level, they were as out of place as I was. They must have formed millions of years ago when this area was below water. As the earth pushed the Himalayan range higher and higher, the fossils remained.

I hadn't expected fossils. Yet, there they were. They were a sign of change. Even plateaus themselves are not permanent. They change, as do we.

It was yet another reminder of how different the reality was from my expectations. My other presuppositions about how I would feel about this place were also wrong.

I had wanted so badly to be here — but now, though my body was still adapting, it was also telling me it wanted to go back down. It wanted to drop back down to the Tibetan Plateau at 14,000 feet, where I hadn't wanted to be but where breathing was easier.

Then I smiled to myself and thought, *this base camp is also the next plateau for those on a journey to the summit.*

I found this place uncomfortable, but for others who were able to go higher, this place would be one of rest and reflection. If I stayed long enough, it would become comfortable for me, too. But right now, all I could think about was getting back down to comfort, where I could breathe more easily.

And I didn't have time to adapt. We were only planning to be there for the day. Tomorrow, we would hike away to a different plateau with new challenges.

The next morning, we hiked back down to the lower camp and met our guides, who were drinking tea in front of

EVEN PLATEAUS
THEMSELVES ARE
NOT PERMANENT.
THEY CHANGE,
AS DO WE.

their tent. Then we started the journey back across the massive Tibetan Plateau — the same one we had left days before.

But now, that plateau seemed different. Not only did I have a different feeling about it, I also had a different view of plateaus in general, both literally and figuratively. I realized that traveling them happened in phases. By knowing what to expect, we can better plan the journey.

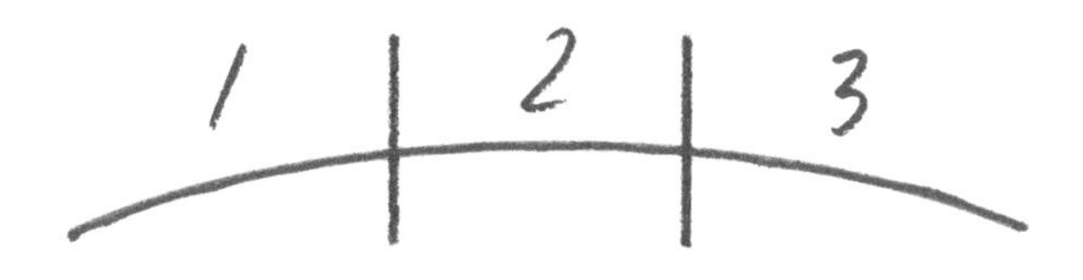

THE THREE PHASES OF THE PLATEAU

In his book *Life Is in the Transitions: Mastering Change at Any Age,* Bruce Feiler explains that you spend nearly half of your life in the transition phases between life events. Those transitions can last up to five years. You're constantly jumping from plateau to plateau, and life itself triggers these jumps.[5]

Feiler discusses the life disruptions that can trigger a Plateau Jump. He mentions everything from changes in employment to finances, relationships, housing, health, and so on.

Feiler didn't call it a Plateau Jump; he called them phases. However, moving through the landscape, I realized how similar these phases are to the plateaus. Feiler says each new phase causes disorientation at first, followed by a reorientation to the new normal, and finally, what he calls a "new orientation" as you gain command over the new circumstances.

Sitting at the Mount Everest base camp, I experienced disorientation. I didn't have time to reorient to the "new normal." If I had stayed, my lungs would have adapted. Altitude is just one type of adjustment one makes on a new plateau, but it's a good metaphor.

You're forever dealing with "life disruptions," as Feiler calls them. The next plateau may not automatically be better, but it will be different.

Where possible, it's important to purposefully choose the next plateau and make it better than the last. How it will be better is up to you to decide.

Remember in Nancy and Harry's situation, when we needed to figure out where they were in their lives to know where they needed to go? To do that, it helps to see the bigger landscape. Recognizing and embracing the three distinct phases of the plateau can help you answer the question of where you are starting from right now. I have seen this in the businesses I have coached and in the personal changes I have worked through with individuals.

Based on my observations, I like to call these phases the Cliffside, the Campground, and the Canyon Wall. Let's take a look at them in more depth.

THE CLIFFSIDE – NEW ENERGIES BRING MOTIVATION

The Cliffside is full of excitement. You've just scaled the cliff, and now you stand on the edge at the top, looking back. Your perspective shifts as you take in not just the distance you've traveled but also the magnitude of your climb. Each breath carries a sense of accomplishment, easing the physical exertion of the ascent. You've reached your goal.

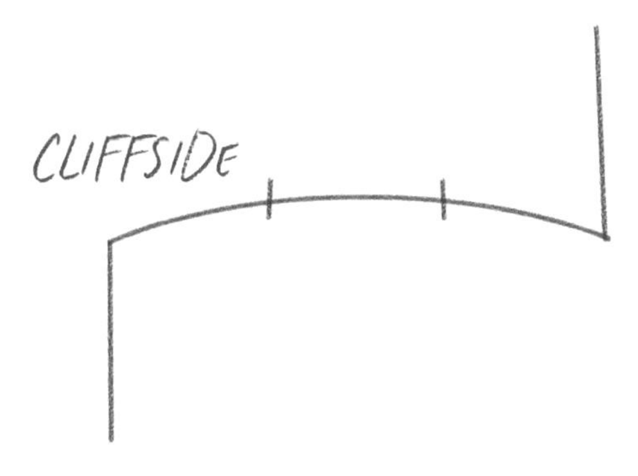

Turning around, you're gifted a panorama that previously remained unseen, shrouded by the challenge of the climb. The proximity of the edge, though, hints at a dangerous reversal, causing you to inch away from the cliff. You retreat to a safer distance from the edge, careful not to let the victorious moment turn into a slip down the steep face you've just scaled.

Cliffside Benefits

The Cliffside comes with several rewards and positive qualities:

- A heightened sense of optimism, motivation, and satisfaction as you embark on new endeavors or make positive changes
- Anticipation of rewards
- The thrill of exploring uncharted territory
- The initial benefits or successes that come with the recent changes and achievements

However, sometimes these things are difficult to cope with, and sometimes, things don't go as hoped.

Make the Most of the Cliffside

The key to the Cliffside is to enjoy the surge of energy from achieving the goal but also to avoid becoming dependent on it or letting the new situation overwhelm you. In many ways, that requires preparation. But it is crucial.

Imagine achieving a major change in your life. One you worked for, such as a new job promotion, a better beach body, or a level of competency in your chosen field or hobby. But then, it all goes away. You get demoted, you let your health slide, your skills in a favorite hobby atrophy. All lost. You'd be devastated. You would find yourself on a new plateau. One you had perhaps ascended from only to now return to.

It takes discipline and awareness not to let this happen — as well as the ability to change your mindset. We'll explore all of these elements in the next chapters. Meanwhile, let's move into the next phase: the Campground.

THE CAMPGROUND – ROUTINE CREATES COMPETENCY AND ADVANCEMENT

The day's exertion, a relentless march through wilderness, has been rewarded with a momentary break from the relentless pursuit of forward progress. The journey to this spot has been a labor, a testament to your tenacity and endurance.

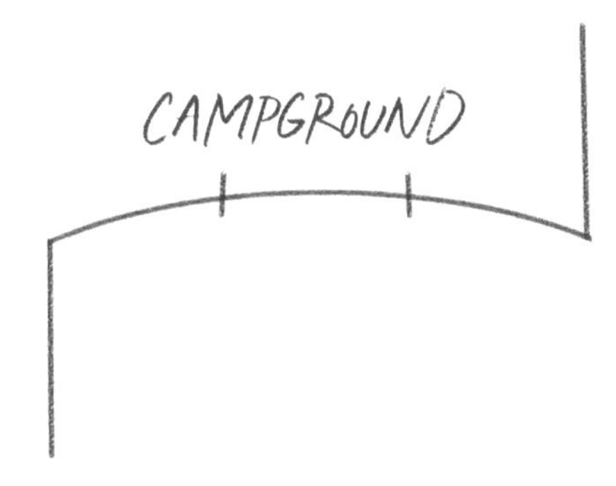

As you approach the Campground, your energy may increase slightly. I have run several marathons, and I have observed that the runners who are slogging along at mile twenty-two seem to find energy for the final half mile of the race.

How is it that this final stretch of a marathon becomes easier? As we approach our goals, connecting with our vision juices us with energy. Watch for this. It is a sign you are nearing your goal and entering the next phase.

As you reach the Campground, your first thought is to unburden yourself, place your backpack against the sturdy trunk of a nearby tree, and surrender to the desire for much-needed rest. But, for the immediate future, your attention is drawn to the practicalities of setting up camp. There's something captivating about this spot, an allure amplified by the picturesque view it offers.

Campground Benefits

When I think about someone thriving in the Campground, I think of engaging in meaningful work. The term "meaningful work" does not need to be limited to employment. It means pursuing and striving for growth. This includes:

- Rest and comfort
- A place to contemplate the journey — where you've been and where you're going
- Continued energy and productivity
- A feeling of success and purpose

For now, in this transient window of time, this place is your own slice of paradise, and it can bring you many positive rewards. The key is to make the most of it.

Because, when we forget to grow, the Canyon Wall awaits.

THE CANYON WALL – GETTING STUCK

Roused from the temporary peace of the campsite, you've been threading through a tapestry of rugged landscapes. It's been arduous and taxing in a way you didn't anticipate. Your mind has been uncharacteristically elsewhere, your attention wandering away from the task at hand, your course absent of clear direction. Perhaps, as I did on my Pacific Crest Trail hike, you've been mindlessly following in someone else's footsteps, thinking that will get you where you want to go.

The trail has twisted and forked, a labyrinth of earth and stone, pulling you deeper into its maze. You followed the meandering paths without much thought, fooled by the illusion of progress, the perceived necessity of momentum. The sense of where you're coming from has blurred, dissolved into what you've mistakenly called "progress."

WHEN WE

FORGET TO GROW,

THE CANYON

WALL AWAITS.

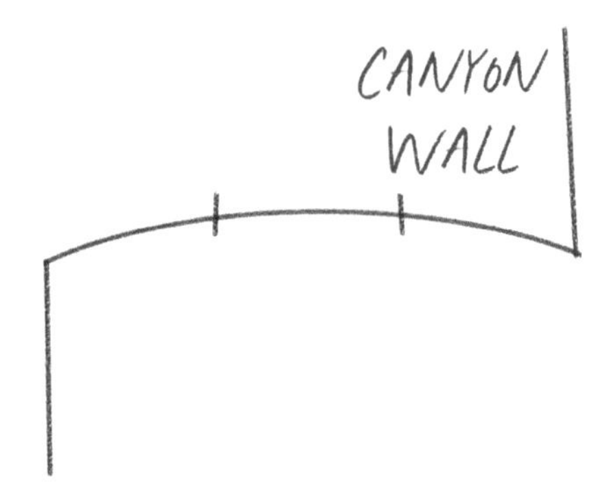

Suddenly, you find yourself at a dead end. A solid rock wall stands before you, formidably marking the canyon's terminus. One look at the monolith paints a grim picture of your climbing prospects. Stepping back for a wider view does nothing but amplify the reality of your predicament. You step back even further, with no better result as you view the colossal edifice before you.

The gnawing reality that you've taken a misstep settles in.

Retracing your steps is now the only option. Your mind stirs with a yearning for the tranquility of your previous Campground.

Canyon Wall Characteristics

When you're at the Canyon Wall, it's difficult to find anything you can call a benefit. You'll know you're there when everything seems to be going wrong:

- You feel stuck or overwhelmed, and you wonder what happened. Everything was going along swimmingly, and then it just stopped working.

- You try new things, but they don't seem to work.
- External forces are pushing unwanted change upon you, and you long for the good ol' days of the Campground when life was easy and energy was abundant.
- Growth has come to a standstill, leaving you feeling trapped and disheartened. The world is moving on. You start losing ground, and things no longer just feel stuck — now, they're deteriorating.

DEALING WITH THE CANYON WALL

This third phase of the plateau, the Canyon Wall, is the most challenging and uncomfortable. The only positive aspect of it is being able to leave it without too much loss. We'll talk about how to do that more in Chapter 3 when we look into the challenges of the different phases. However, here are some suggestions that can help you cope as you move back to the more comfortable state of the Campground.

- **Monitor your awareness:** Regularly evaluate your awareness to ensure you are staying on track and making progress toward your short-term goals.
- **Recognize the signs of distress:** The first step in addressing distress is to be aware of its presence. Look for symptoms such as decreased motivation, fatigue, or feelings of being overwhelmed. Mindfulness exercises, such as meditation or deep breathing, can help alleviate distress and improve mental focus. These practices have been shown to

reduce anxiety and enhance cognitive functioning, allowing for clearer evaluation of decisions.

- **Find social support:** Seek out mentors, role models, or groups who have successfully navigated similar challenges and learn from their experiences and strategies. Social support acts as a buffer against stress, reducing its negative impact on decision-making processes.
- **Direct your energy:** Be proactive in seeking out new opportunities for growth and advancement, whether through additional training or education, new projects or responsibilities at work, or personal interests and hobbies. Those activities should move you closer to your next plateau. Concentrate your efforts on areas within your control or influence; spend no energy on areas where you have no control.

RETURNING FROM THE TIBETAN PLATEAU

As my daughter, Summer, and I hiked back down the rocky trail from Everest Base Camp, breathing became easier. I shouldered Summer's backpack to lighten her load.

Oh, and my own pack was a little heavier with the weight of a small fossil — a souvenir to remind me that we must reach our next plateau to gain new insights about what we may find there. Sometimes, what we find may surprise us. If you look, if you seek, and if you pursue, you can find the unexpected.

Within each phase lies hidden lessons on how to navigate change with precision — to initiate change before it initiates itself. That is the essence of Plateau Jumping.

IF YOU LOOK,

IF YOU SEEK,

AND IF YOU PURSUE,

YOU CAN FIND

THE UNEXPECTED.

In the next chapter, we will explore how to deal with the challenges and dangers that hinder our progress in each phase so we can become more effective Plateau Jumpers.

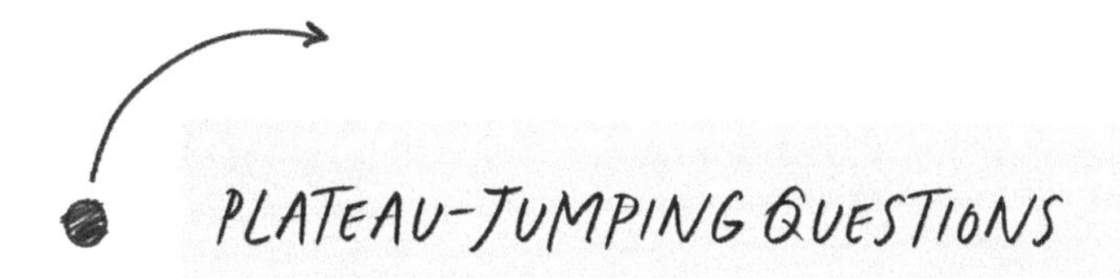

PLATEAU-JUMPING QUESTIONS

What phase of the plateau do you think you are on? Why do you think that?

What does directing your attention to the next plateau look like for you?

What are the distractions that could pull your energy and attention away from your next plateau?

CHAPTER 3

Surmounting the Challenges

PREPARATION JUMPS THE UNEXPECTED

"Comfort is the enemy of progress." — P.T. BARNUM, SHOWMAN

"When you come out of the storm, you won't be the same person who walked in. That's what the storm is all about." — HARUKI MURAKAMI

WHEN I WAS a young boy, I lived briefly in New Mexico. I remember hearing a Native-American-themed story about a Navajo boy who went out hunting one day. He was chasing after a rabbit and, in the process, got himself trapped. The rabbit jumped down the edge of a small cliff to escape. The boy, carelessly focused only on pursuit, followed. He jumped down from a high plateau in the desert to a lower one, where he had seen the rabbit dash to escape. Once he found himself on the lower plateau, he was stuck. The rabbit he chased was now gone. As much as he tried, he couldn't jump high enough to get back up from where he had jumped down.

He remained on this plateau until one day, watching a hawk circle high above him, he prayed to the spirits, grew wings, and flew. While aloft, high above his temporary prison of the lower plateau, he noticed an escape off the plateau where he had been trapped. A hidden trail had been there the whole time — an exit that would have led him home. He hadn't seen the solution from that inopportune lower plateau's vantage point. He needed to simply have faith and perspective and then jump to get to where he wanted to go.

Although she claims to not remember, my mother probably made that story up on the spot as she tried to put me to sleep. Wherever it originated, it was more layered than I could appreciate at the time. But its essence stayed with me.

The boy had found himself in an unfamiliar place without a clear idea of how to get out or even how he got there. From his vantage point, he seemed stuck. Only by getting a different perspective could he realize he hadn't really been stuck. The answer is always there if you look for it in different ways.

Each phase of the landscape comes with its inherent challenges. Some are more easily spotted than others, but that might mean the ones you don't suspect will be the ones that end up being the hardest to overcome, mainly because you weren't prepared for them.

Let's look at the dangers in each phase in a little more detail here and explore how to get through them.

A CLIFFSIDE TRAGEDY: *WISH YOU WERE HERE...* FROM SHADOWS TO STARDOM AND BACK

In the mid-1960s, a young musician named Syd Barrett emerged from the smoky depths of London's underground music scene. His haunting melodies and voice captivated the few fortunate enough to hear him perform. Little did they know that he would become a catalyst for a musical revolution, forever altering the course of rock history.

Born Roger Barrett in Cambridge, England,[6] the young artist possessed extraordinary talent. His voice resonated with a unique quality; his lyrics painted vivid landscapes of emotion. However, it wasn't until Barrett united with kindred spirits that his true journey commenced.

As he formed his band, Barrett's vision guided them toward uncharted territories. The band's sound evolved, captivating listeners' imaginations and catapulting the group to commercial success. One of their early breakthrough hits climbed the charts, and record stores struggled to keep up with the demand for their albums. The band's ascent was as thrilling as it was unexpected. The band, Pink Floyd, began to permeate the public consciousness.

But it was with their follow-up single, "See Emily Play,"[7] that Pink Floyd's star burned brightest. The psychedelic anthem soared through the airwaves, ascending to the upper echelons of the charts. Barrett's kaleidoscopic visions were crystallized in the song's mesmerizing melody and mind-bending lyrics. It reached an impressive number six on the charts, solidifying Pink Floyd's status as pioneers of the psychedelic movement. Barrett's energy and magnetism had helped the band reach the next plateau.

Unfortunately, he would have a tough time staying there. He was balanced precariously on the Cliffside.

As the band's star ascended, Barrett grappled with the weight of his newfound success. The blinding glare of fame clashed with his introverted nature, and the pressure began to engulf him. Uncomfortable with the meteoric rise, he sought refuge back in obscurity. Barrett and Pink Floyd were not destined to occupy the spotlight together for much longer.

As time passed, Barrett's heavy use of psychedelic drugs, particularly LSD, resulted in his downward spiral into mental instability. He became increasingly withdrawn, experiencing hallucinations, disorganized speech, memory lapses, and intense mood swings.[8] The once joyful artist began to exhibit a blank, dead-eyed stare, failing to recognize friends and often losing awareness of his surroundings. During performances, his erratic behavior became pronounced, strumming a single chord throughout an entire concert or standing motionless, arms by his sides, staring into the abyss of his own mind.

Faced with a heart-wrenching decision born out of love for their music and their collective desire to continue their sonic exploration, the band was forced to replace Barrett with guitarist David Gilmour, recognizing his talent and dedication as the key to carrying Pink Floyd into the future.[9] The painful decision meant severing ties not only with one of the band's founders but also with their leader and creative inspiration. He was the one who had sparked their artistic revolution. Yet, they knew they had to forge ahead, honoring the legacy they had built together.

The decision to replace Barrett proved pivotal, allowing them to continue making their mark on the world of music while forever cherishing the initial impact of their inspirational bandmate.

In 1975, as Pink Floyd gathered in the studio, anticipation hung in the air. They were recording the album *Wish You Were Here*[10]. The album, dedicated to Barrett, is a poignant tribute to their former bandmate. The composition titled "Shine on You Crazy Diamond" encapsulated the soaring heights and haunting depths of Barrett's musical genius. It was a song that dealt with the rise to fame, the isolation, and the loss of the brilliance that was the essence of Syd himself.

Meanwhile, in the recording booth, an unannounced, overweight man with a shaved head and eyebrows stood silently, observing the band with a far-off gaze. As the final notes of the songs filled the air, the band recognized the man: Before them, bearing the weight of his own journey, was Syd Barrett himself, the now nearly unrecognizable genius they had once revered.[11]

Pink Floyd went on to be inducted into the Rock and Roll Hall of Fame in 1996. Barrett was listed as a member but was noticeably absent. He passed away in 2006, having largely retreated from the public eye and never having maintained the level of achievement he had first reached with his fellow band members.

Avoiding the Cliffside Dangers: Sliding Back to False Comfort

When people make radical or meaningful changes in their lives, they can feel optimized and energized at first. However, the danger is that one will lose energy and get overwhelmed. When this happens, it's tempting to fall back into old habits.

In their book *Systems of Psychotherapy: A Transtheoretical Analysis*, James Prochaska and John Norcross call this phenomenon "relapse,"[12] and it is one of the several challenges at the Cliffside:

- Relapse into old, unproductive behaviors
- A tendency to look back nostalgically on "the good old days" (even when they weren't as good as you remember)
- The undoing of recent achievements

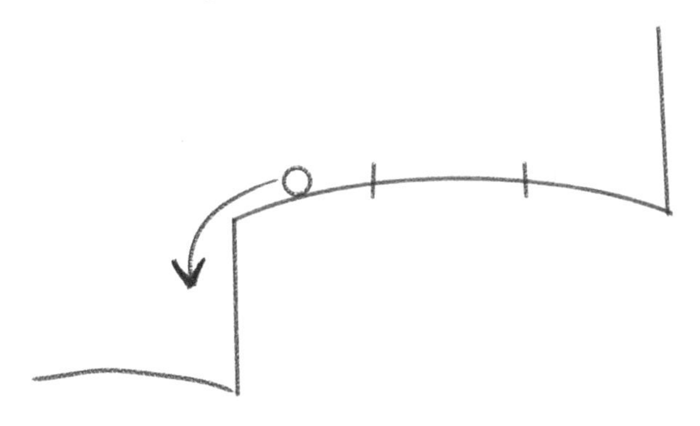

Why does this happen? The stress of the new situation creates internal conflict, and conflict is uncomfortable. "Let's get back to where it is comfortable," you think. You stop working diligently in your job, you stop working out, you stop practicing the new skill you've been trying to learn. You want to go back to how it used to be, even if how it used to be wasn't really better.

The stress can also come when you've moved upward too quickly — remember my altitude sickness at the base camp of Mount Everest? I was uncomfortable and unprepared, wanting to get back down quickly. When you are unprepared, this is a common response.

We can backslide even if our lives literally depend on making new changes. For instance, a team of researchers from Harvard Medical School published a study in the *Journal of General Internal Medicine* in 2018 that followed heart-attack survivors over a period of six years.[13] Researchers tracked their progress in terms of lifestyle changes, such as eating a healthier diet, exercising regularly, and quitting smoking.

While many of the heart-attack survivors made significant progress in the first few months after their cardiac event, the vast majority eventually reverted to their old, unhealthy habits. In fact, by the end of the study, only 1 percent of the participants were following all the recommended lifestyle changes.

This study highlights the fact that even when people receive clear and direct feedback about the positive impact of their actions, they may still struggle to maintain those behaviors over the long term.

But the Cliffside isn't the only place where things can go downhill. Though the Campground has its share of comforts, under those lie a different set of dangers.

A CAMPGROUND DILEMMA: FROM POTATO CHIPS TO MICROCHIPS

You may not know J.R. Simplot's name, but it's certain you know what he sold.

Simplot began as a simple potato farmer. He was also a brilliant entrepreneur. He got his start in the potato industry in Idaho during the Great Depression. It didn't take long to become one of the largest potato farmers in the state and eventually the oldest billionaire on the Forbes 400.[14]

The entrepreneur in him wanted to find a way to make more money from his potatoes than just selling them fresh or as potato chips. Simplot began to experiment with freeze-drying techniques in the 1940s. Freeze-drying involves removing the water from a product to extend its shelf life. This is a tricky process for potatoes — trickier than it may seem. At the time, freeze-drying was not yet perfected and was too expensive to be practical.

Despite the challenges, Simplot persisted and developed a way to freeze-dry potatoes. The approach his company developed was both cost-effective and practical. This breakthrough allowed him to sell potatoes year-round. Up until then, only certain types of potatoes were available during certain parts of the year. This created difficulty for food suppliers and restaurants that wanted to sell French fries year-round. This is where the story starts to get good for Simplot.

One big customer saw the ability to sell French fries year-round as a massive growth opportunity. That customer was McDonald's. Soon, Simplot was the primary supplier of frozen potatoes to the largest seller of French fries in the world.[15] He quickly became a rich man.

Imagine yourself in a situation where you've achieved rapid, robust success. You've gone from monitoring nickels and dimes to being over-resourced. Your decision-making might not be as thorough as before when finances were tight. You might adopt a different, less creative mindset now that problems can be solved by money. Your attention may drift away from your purpose.

We could assume that Simplot may have fallen into any of these traps. Business practices began to get sloppy. Legal troubles came a few years later. Simplot was charged with tax fraud for not reporting more than $1 million in corporate income and claiming false personal and family deductions.[16] He pleaded *nolo contendere* ("no contest), saying, "... I've never done anything wrong that I know of."

When you are comfortable, it becomes easy to let things slide. It becomes easy to get complacent and assume systems that have worked will keep working. If you are not diligent, skills will atrophy, competitive edges can disappear, and external pressures will push you out of that comfort zone. Simplot was pushed out of the Campground and found himself against the Canyon Wall.

In 1980, when Simplot was seventy-one, he decided to move away from the Canyon Wall back to the Campground and jump to a new plateau. He got business back in order. Then he took a gamble on two young entrepreneurs, Ward and Joe Parkinson.

They had founded a semiconductor company called Micron Technology Inc. A computer memory-chip manufacturer, Micron was struggling to find funds to take its business to the next level. Simplot saw potential in the brothers and made a venture capital deal with them for a 40 percent stake in the company.[17] Little did he know that this investment would become the most successful decision of his life.

Simplot's investment in Micron was a significant risk, but he recognized the potential of the semiconductor industry and believed that the company could succeed with the right management and leadership.

His investment paid off. Micron became a leading producer of memory chips and one of the largest semiconductor companies in the world. Its founders became billionaires, and Simplot made his second fortune.

Simplot had faced adversity in his personal and professional life. There must have been an inescapable temptation to bask in the comfort of The Campground. His investment in Micron was an example of his willingness to jump at opportunity — to jump to the next plateau.

Simplot passed away in 2008 at the age of ninety-nine, but his legacy lives on. It tells us to be willing to make a jump from the Campground even if we are jumping all the way from potato chips to microchips.

The Dangers of the Campground: Complacency and Demotivation

In the Campground, you may fantasize about staying indefinitely. But a realistic part of you acknowledges the finite nature of your supplies, the uncompromising rule of survival that necessitates forward motion. The world will change, too. A lingering stay beyond your time is a luxury you can't afford.

How do you know it's your time to leave? You may be so focused on the Campground that you don't notice what is happening:

- The powerful motivating force that invigorated your journey up to the Cliffside can begin to fade. Progress starts to gradually slow and may even stop.
- What used to work no longer gets the desired results.
- You may become focused only on the comforts and rewards of the Campground, not on moving or growing further.
- Unaware of the changing forces of nature around you, you may find yourself forced to leave the Campground without enough preparation.

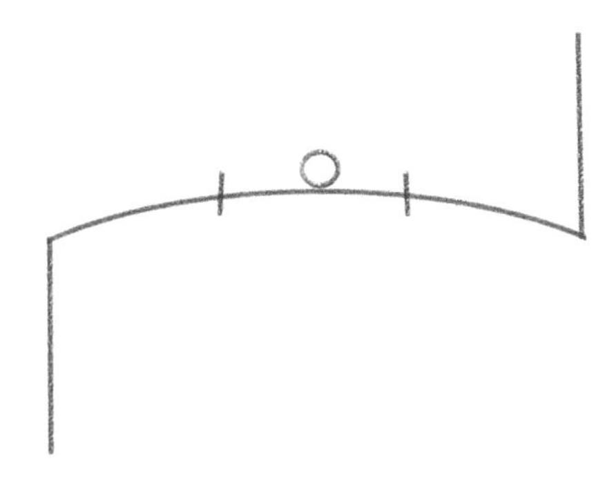

You'll notice a similarity with the problems at the Canyon Wall, and that's no mistake. The Canyon Wall's problems start at the Campground.

In the Campground, complacency is the greatest challenge. It's easy to slip into routines without enough creativity. Like Simplot, you can start to lose your edge. You become too comfortable, and your progress stagnates. In the Campground, complacency makes it easy to find yourself back on the Cliffside, where you could backslide even further, landing at a previous plateau.

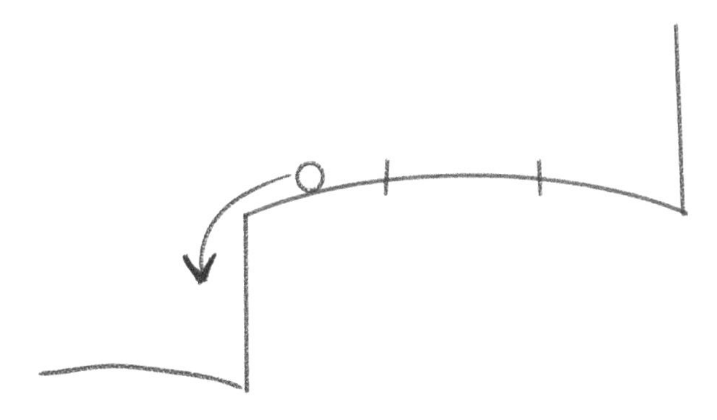

However, it is just as easy to slide forward and get trapped in the increasing complexity and challenges of the Canyon Wall, where you have to face the changing landscape before you're ready. At the far edge of the Campground, the things you are doing no longer seem to be having the impact they once did. You start to notice you're no longer making the progress or growth rate you once enjoyed. Achievement of meaningful goals seems to be becoming just out of reach.

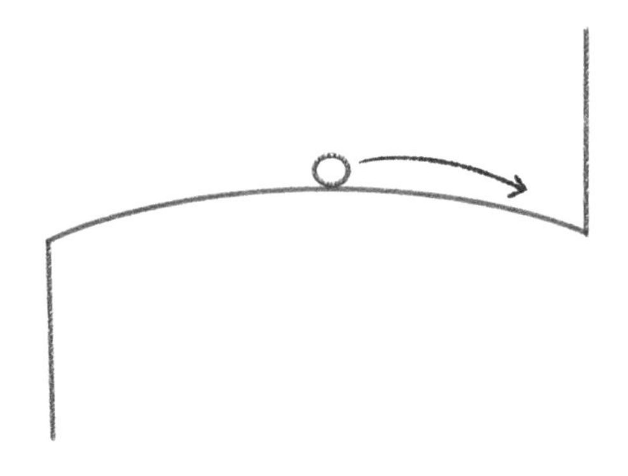

The Comfort Zone: Use It Wisely

To prevent stagnation, it is important to embrace the Campground as a time for reflection, evaluation, and new goal-setting. It seems counterintuitive, but this place of comfort and rest is the very spot from which to initiate change.

We are built for constant growth and exploration. The lack of motivation you feel upon reaching the Campground can be rekindled when you decide on a new goal.

A few years ago, I was coaching a group of financial advisors in Denver and asked an introductory question. "What do you hope to get from our time together?"

The first to respond was an older man who said he wanted to challenge himself and get out of his comfort zone. This was a typical response based on my subject matter. I wrote it on the board up front.

The next answer was from a younger financial advisor sitting up front. "First, I just want to get *into* my comfort zone!"

Both of these answers sum up our relationship with the Campground. We are constantly moving into or out of a comfort zone. That comfort zone is where we can clearly assess the next plateau. And eventually, the comfort zone will *be* that next plateau.

True to this statement, roughly ten years later, that younger advisor was standing on stage at his company's national conference, having led the nation in sales. He was several comfort zones away from where he'd started.

The key is to be ready to move when it's time.

Why is the Campground a perfect place to make new plans?

- It is the place on the plateau with the maximum number of resources and personal energy. Planning takes time and thought. At the Campground, you have time to think.
- If we have the right mindset, the Campground's stable, comfortable environment is the very thing that can help us avoid feeling stuck. Research has found that the right competitive environment, one that is fair and has winnable odds, will even motivate some to continue to strive for success.[18]

So, here in the Campground, it is time to take stock and set your sights on what is next. If you do this, you can avoid the problems you'll encounter in the next phase, the Canyon Wall, entirely. As we've seen in Chapter 2, the Canyon Wall is not the place you want to find yourself unexpectedly, especially when you're not prepared to deal with its challenges.

A CANYON WALL HORROR STORY: STUCK BETWEEN A ROCK AND A HARD PLACE

My son Sanger and I lowered ourselves into the deep crevasse. Cold glacial melt was dripping onto our ropes and harnesses, drenching everything we were wearing. The deep blue glacier ice inside the Davidson Glacier was as pure blue as we had ever seen.

We were there at the Alaskan site with our guide, Evan, for a three-day ice-climbing trip. We were to go up and into the Davidson Glacier. The day before, we kayaked across Chilkoot Inlet, pulled our kayaks into the woods, and hiked the rest of the way for a few miles to the foot of the massive glacier. The long hike, carrying all our provisions and climbing gear, took us past three massive brown bears and through 7,293 mosquitoes.[19]

We spent this particular morning strapping crampons (spiked devices used to get traction on ice and snow) to our boots and using them to climb up the glacier, kicking hard to jam the spikes into the vertical wall of ice. With our ice axes, we slowly lifted ourselves up, bit by bit.

Once we reached a small resting spot up on top, we admired the beauty of Chilkoot Inlet from our glacial vantage point.

Evan broke the silence. "You know, I met a guy a couple of years ago when I was ice climbing in Colorado. This guy had a prosthetic arm with a freakin' ice axe attached!" He held up his own ice axe to punctuate the statement.

"What?! He was climbing like that?!" Sanger and I questioned, still feeling the effects of our own short climb in our arms and legs.

"Yeah, this dude was just goin'," Evan recalled. "Pullin' himself right up with that damn thing. It was amazing!"

That "dude," as it turned out, was Aron Ralston. Ralston knows a thing or two about canyon walls. An experienced climber, he has reached the summit of every fourteen-thousand-foot-high peak in Colorado (the "fourteeners") solo — in the winter. Although that feat alone would gain Ralston respect among local mountaineering circles, in May of 2003, he met fame for something different. Something unwanted.

During a solo hike through Utah's Bluejohn Canyon, Ralston came to a canyon wall. As he ascended the wall just like he had done many times before, a boulder shifted, pinning his right wrist.

With no way to lift the boulder, chisel it away, or work his hand loose, Ralston was pinned to the wall for six excruciating days. Getting up and over that canyon wall would take something neither Ralston nor many others would want to imagine.

Near the end of his six-day ordeal, after exhausting his food rations and all other options, time was running out. Being "between a rock and a hard place" was not just a figure of speech; it was a literal description of his situation and would later become his book's title.[20]

With his pocketknife, he carefully cut the skin, muscles, and tendons above his wrist. The cuts severed nerves and shot electrical impulses through his body. Then, with only the bone exposed, he jerked what was left of his arm. With a hard, loud snap, he broke the bones in his forearm, pulled away, and freed himself at last from his stuck hand, the bolder, and the canyon wall.

The Canyon Wall: Extreme Emotions Deplete Reserves

It's likely you will never get stuck at life's Canyon Wall in such an extreme situation as Ralston did. Still, finding yourself at the Canyon Wall in any situation is no picnic. The Canyon Wall is the least desirable of the three phases and the most challenging. Its dangers come from its extreme situations and their emotional toll:

- The presence of the Canyon Wall is overwhelming, obstructing your view of the next plateau, leaving you no choice but to seek change. You can't climb this wall from here, but maybe you can jump if you back up a bit.

- Distress takes hold, a formidable force that heightens cortisol levels and clouds your judgment, leading to a cascade of poor decisions.

- You're depleting our energy and resources, yet the change you seek starts to get out of reach. As much as you try to constrain it, entropy has stopped conforming to your parameters.

- The deteriorating environment around you makes it harder and harder to initiate the change to grow and advance. You want to do something, but you don't know what you can do or how.

When you find yourself stuck in this kind of situation, the biggest key is not to panic.

How to Avoid the Canyon Wall

The best way to prevent getting stuck on the Canyon Wall is to avoid getting near it in the first place.

Be Aware

If you're aware, you'll see the Canyon Wall before it traps you. You'll avoid getting stuck. You'll begin to make the moves to get back to the Campground before you get close enough to the Canyon Wall to get trapped.

Focus on What You Can Control

One problem with the Canyon Wall is that it creates more and more emotional stress that impedes decision-making. How do you combat that?

One of the guests we had on the Decidedly podcast was author and Hindu priest Dandapani.[21] In his book *The Power of Unwavering Focus,*[22] Dandapani discusses how our awareness can drift to places in our minds. He says it is our role to become aware of this and to redirect that focus.

He makes the point that where our focus goes, our energy flows. If you notice that you are focusing on the negatives of the Canyon Wall, redirect your attention back to changing the things you can change. Multiple forces put you into the Canyon Wall; some you can control, some you can only influence, and others you have neither influence nor control over. You can control your own focus, which should, in turn, be centered around only those forces you control. Spend zero time lamenting the external forces that you have no control over changing.

Focus on the Goal Itself — Get Back to the Campground

Focusing on what you're trying *to do* vs. what you're trying *not to do* is crucial. I learned this from a friend of mine, and it's stuck with me ever since.

Chipping from off the green, Jeremy Poincenot[23] won the golf tournament that branded him a world champion in the sport. Jeremy didn't see the shot that caused the crowd to cheer for him. He hadn't seen any of the shots that day. He hadn't seen any of his golf shots that would bring him recognition since age nineteen when he lost his sight.

Jeremy has a rare genetic disorder called Leber's Hereditary Optic Neuropathy (LHON). It began to impact his sight during a semester in college, and before that semester was over, Jeremy was blind. The tournament he won was the 2010 World Blind Golf Championship.

Golf is challenging enough, but as a blind golfer, Jeremy deals with added challenges that change the game. It becomes a two-person sport involving the golfer and a guide. The guide pinpoints the goal and lines up the directionality and distance of the shots. That goal could be the flag waving in the wind sitting at the front of the green or the fairway spot before a dogleg to the right, 185 yards away. "A little to the left — no, not that much," they'll suggest.

Jeremy and I had a chance to hit a few golf balls a few years ago at a course in Fort Worth, and I spotted for him as he crushed his shots down the fairway. At one point, I was describing the hole in front of us. "Ok, now we are aiming for the flag on the right, not the other one off to the far left." I didn't want him to hit onto the other fairway, as I tend to do.

"Shawn, if I could see the other fairway, I wouldn't need you to guide me," he said, ribbing me a little. "Don't tell me about anything but the goal. Everything else is irrelevant. I can't see those things."

Blindness isn't usually considered a benefit, but in this case, he had an unusual advantage over me in that he could pinpoint his focus. We often get distracted by things that aren't the goal. Jeremy had made a point to me beyond golf, and he knew it.

All you need to do is focus on what you are trying to achieve — not on what you are trying *not* to achieve. As Dandapani said, where your awareness goes, energy flows. Keep your awareness only on the goal. If awareness drifts, move it back.

Getting Out of the Trap

But if you do become trapped on the Canyon Wall, like Ralston, you must sever that which pins you down. Ralston's problem was easy to determine; accepting and implementing the solution was the challenge. Your own trap could be more difficult to identify, yet implementing a solution might be much easier than Ralston's. You could be trapped in a mindset that isn't serving you. You could be trapped in a situation that looked aligned with your objectives but isn't now. You could be trapped by fears or insecurities that won't allow you to move.

Regardless of what your personal trap is, the objectives are the same: Cut loose. Get back to stability.

Then jump.

DEALING WITH THE DIFFERENT TYPES OF STRESS

You may have noticed that each distinct phase comes with its own set of accompanying stresses that are more prevalent there. They are unique in their character and how they impact you.

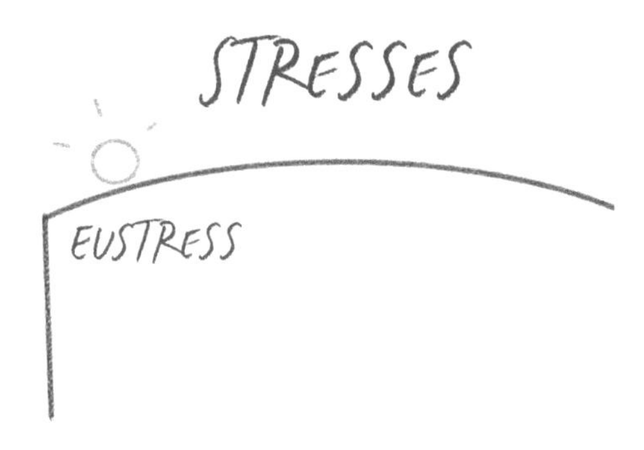

Eustress: "Good Stress"

When we are meeting our goals and feeling great, such as when we've just reached the top of the Cliffside, that doesn't mean there is an absence of stress. The stress is just different. In this case, it's called "eustress." The term comes from the Greek prefix "eu-", which means "good," and the English word "stress." It was coined by the endocrinologist Hans Selye, who also introduced the concept of "stress" as we now understand it in the biological and psychological sense.[24]

Eustress refers to a positive form of stress that can benefit the individual. It is the stress you feel when you're excited or challenged in a good way, like when you're starting a new job, moving to a new city, or waiting to start a race. Eustress can motivate you, improve your performance, and even boost your physical and mental health. In fact, research has shown that experiencing eustress can lead to increased productivity and better health outcomes.[25] It is that feeling of anticipation and excitement before a big presentation. It is the adrenaline rush before a competition.

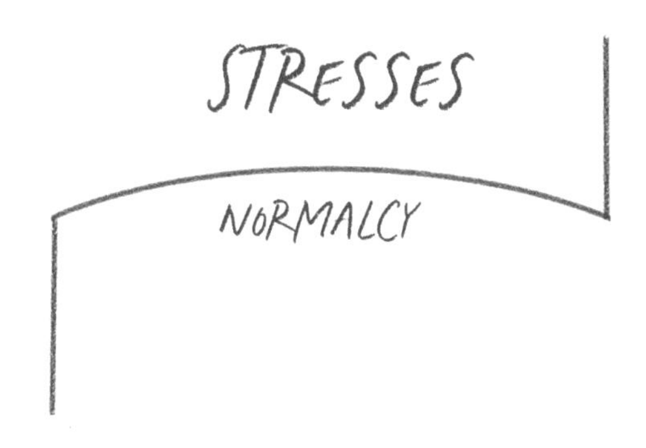

Normalcy: "Routine Stress"

Normalcy is the type of stress found at the Campground phase. It can become so routine that you don't even notice it. It's the stress of commuting to work, completing tasks on a deadline, or managing a busy schedule. While normal stress is a part of everyday life, it's important to recognize that chronic exposure to this type of stress can lead to negative health outcomes.[26]

The Biosphere2 sits in the Arizona desert as a living lab to discover the workings of the world we live in. It is a self-contained environment of nature growing everything from food crops to coral reefs. Scientists observe the effects of the controlled environment to test the viability of an enclosed environment.

A few years ago, as the scientists sought to recreate a rainforest biome, they planted several trees native to the rainforest. With the optimal amount of sunlight, temperatures, and water, they flourished. They grew much faster and taller than in nature.

And then, they fell over.

Without the wind buffering them, they grew roots that were insubstantial.[27] They had not developed stress wood. In trees, stress wood, or reaction wood, is a type of specialized wood that forms in response to mechanical stress, usually due to gravity, wind, or other external forces. It helps the trees withstand those stresses by reorienting themselves to achieve optimal growth. Turns out the trees needed a little bit of stress to thrive. So do we.

In the hustle and bustle of our everyday lives, normal stress quietly weaves its way into our existence. Though not debilitating, it possesses the power to subtly shape our experiences. Like an ever-present companion, stress influences our emotions, thoughts, and behaviors, leaving its mark on our well-being. It whispers in our ears, heightening our awareness and sharpening our focus.

There are the obvious downsides of too much unrelenting stress, even if it's normal. By becoming more mindful of normal stress and developing effective coping strategies, you manage this stress, grow strong from it, and prevent it from becoming chronic.

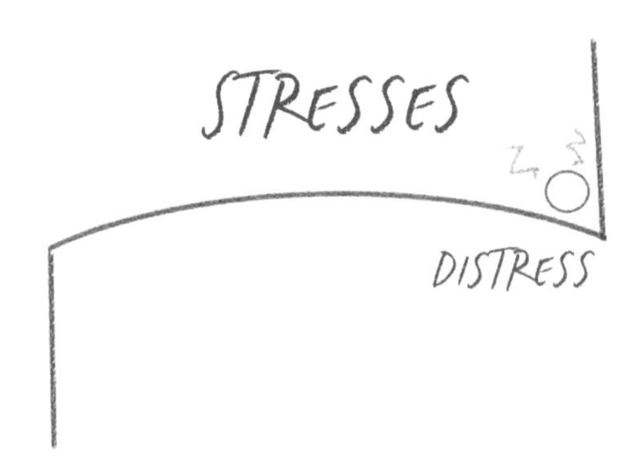

Distress: "Harmful Stress"

Hans Selye used the term "distress" to refer to harmful or negative stress, like the stress we feel when we're under too much pressure or facing insurmountable challenges.[28] It's what you face at the Canyon Wall. It's the stress that comes from traumatic experiences, financial hardship, or chronic illness.

When under distress, your body's stress response can go into overdrive, resulting in high levels of stress hormones like cortisol and adrenaline. These high levels can harm the body over the long term, causing problems such as increased risk for heart disease, hypertension, diabetes, mental health disorders, and more. Unlike eustress, which can be motivating and improve performance, distress typically decreases performance and can negatively affect one's overall quality of life. Chronic exposure to distress can lead to increased cortisol levels, decreased cognitive performance and memory function, and negative health outcomes.[29]

Managing Stress = Maximizing Plateau Phases

Stress is inevitable. By recognizing that not all stress is created equal, we can develop effective strategies to manage our stress as we move through the phases of the plateau.

Knowing how to manage the different types of stress is the same thing as maximizing the positive aspects of the landscape. By understanding the dangers of the Cliffside, you will be aware of them and less likely to let stress cause you to backslide. By managing the Campground routines and their normal stress, you'll not only know how to make the most of the Campground, but you'll also know when it's time to jump from the Campground to the next Cliffside and avoid hitting the Canyon Wall. But if you do hit the Canyon Wall, you'll realize why you're so stressed there and have a better chance of getting back to the Campground sooner so you can plan your next jump.

Now that you understand the landscape and its inherent pitfalls, let's take a look at the unique reasons we want to travel it. Because, as you already know, Plateau Jumping has its rewards.

CHAPTER 4

Fueling the Motivations

INTRINSIC JUMPS EXTERNAL

"Success is not the key to happiness. Happiness is the key to success. If you love what you are doing, you will be successful."
— ALBERT SCHWEITZER, PHILOSOPHER

"When you arise in the morning, think of what a precious privilege it is to be alive — to breathe, to think, to enjoy, to love." — MARCUS AURELIUS, ROMAN EMPEROR

STARTING WITH THE proper mindset is crucial in almost any meaningful endeavor you will embark upon. Plateau Jumping is no different.

Being open and adaptable to the changing nature of the landscape and the lessons you can learn there will help prepare you for each new plateau.

Being aware of your true values and motivations and aligning your actions to the same helps direct your energy without diversion. Happiness and satisfaction will not derive from the place you want to be but from the *person you become* from the journey.

HAPPINESS AND
SATISFACTION WILL NOT
DERIVE FROM THE PLACE
YOU WANT TO BE
BUT FROM THE PERSON
YOU BECOME FROM
THE JOURNEY.

ADAPTABILITY: EMBRACING LIFE'S UNEXPECTED TURNS

I introduced you to Nancy and Harry earlier. There is more to their story.

One day, a card came to me in the mail from Nancy. I was surprised, as I was not scheduled to meet with the couple for another few months. Often, she would send me questions or documents to review ahead of our meetings, but this was nothing like that. This was a large pink envelope with "Do Not Bend" written on the outside.

Curious, I sat down at the black granite table in my office and carefully opened the envelope. I smiled when I saw what was inside.

Out of the large, pink envelope spilled photos of waterfalls, flowers, and beaches. Photos from her trip to New Zealand with Harry. They had not told me they were going on the trip, so this was a pleasant surprise.

A nice handwritten letter accompanied the photos — a thank-you note from Nancy. She wrote that our discussion about what was important had motivated them to act. She and Harry had finally taken the trip that they had been talking about for so long. She used that trip to complete the project for the photography class that she had signed up for after our values conversation.

It was rewarding to know our discussion had been meaningful. I saved the thank-you note and photos and made a mental note to tell Nancy how much I appreciated the gesture when I saw them in a couple of months.

When our meeting time arrived, I heard Nancy's voice in the lobby. I came out to greet her, and we walked back to my office and sat down at the black granite table. I launched into how much I appreciated the note and how good the photos were. We chatted about the trip. But she did not match my energy level. Something was off.

"So, where is Harry?" I asked, probably too cheerily.

"Well, that's what I wanted to share with you. You've probably noticed I have been managing the finances for a while." I had noticed, but it didn't seem strange. Nancy had been an account executive before her retirement. Being the more business-minded of the couple, she often oversaw the finances.

"You probably noticed too that Harry has missed the last couple of meetings." I had noticed that, too. Now, I sensed something was coming.

"Harry is sick," she said. "He has been sick for a while, and it's the kind of sick that doesn't get better. Two months ago, he also had a small stroke, and it really set him back."

"I'm so sorry, Nancy."

"I sent you all those photos and the letter because that's the last trip we will take. Harry doesn't leave the house anymore. Which means I rarely leave the house, either. Our daughter is there with him now, so I could come to talk to you. I wanted to thank you because the talk we had with you about values and motivations helped urge Harry into action. He never wanted to spend money on much. When we started talking about being free from worry, I think that made an impact. We realized we could be. We just needed to start acting like it."

Alignment: Living Your Values

In noting our talk about values, Nancy was referring to an exercise we had done when they came into my office for the meeting I've already told you about. That was the year prior, right after I returned from the Pacific Crest Trail.

As part of that meeting, I had a deck of special cards ready. On each of these cards was a personal value with a brief definition.

I asked Nancy and Harry to look through the cards and divide them into two stacks: one stack of values they thought of as "very important" to them and another stack that was just "important."

This was a bit challenging because all the values seemed praiseworthy, but they completed it. Then, I challenged them again. I removed the "Important" stack they had created and focused on the "Very Important" stack.

"Now, from this stack, find those values that rise to the top fifteen," I directed. "This is going to get more difficult because now you've already said they are all 'very important.' But we're looking for the fifteen most important. Remember, you are not rejecting these other values or embracing their opposite. We are just filtering."

From the fifteen, we reduced it to ten, and finally, to five: *Honesty, Faith, Family, Security, and Relationships.*

We talked in depth about each of them. I asked:

- What does this value mean to you?
- What made you select this value?
- How do you see this value manifesting itself in your life?

We talked about what they could be doing to live out each of their values. We talked about *honesty* and how they appreciated me being straightforward with them in having them go through the exercise. We talked about how their *faith* would lead them to start a charitable foundation. We talked about *family* and how they wanted to set up a trust for their grandson. We talked about *security* and restructuring their investments to give them more peace of mind. Finally, we talked about *relationships* and how they wanted to grow closer to each other through shared experiences. That led to the trip to New Zealand.

For most people I talk to, the issue missing in their lives is not that they are acting in conflict with their values. That happens, but far less frequently than we would think.

What happens more often is that they profess a value, yet it has no identifiable outlet. They are not manifesting it in their lives. Their image of themselves does not align with their actions when the rubber meets the road.

After a pause, Nancy spoke again, "When we spoke a year ago, you weren't just convincing me; I had been saying those things to Harry for the past few years. Although it didn't seem like it at the time, you were convincing Harry." We sat in silence for a bit, and then she just said quietly and calmly, "Thank you."

They had made a big jump.

I have included a sample list of values in the appendix for you to use in your own exercise. Try going through the exercise of narrowing down your values, just as I did with Nancy and Harry. When you are down to your five top values, begin to ask yourself how they are manifesting themselves and expressing themselves in your life. Maybe even turn those singular words into statements that express each value in a more personal way.

Ask yourself, "What is the external gift of these values I am giving the world?" This is your action. This is the real you that needs to be acting on the gift of these values you wish to exemplify.

If you find that you have professed values that are not being expressed or lived out, challenge yourself to either re-examine that value or seek a way to express it. Perhaps the expression itself exists on the next plateau.

If it does, jump.

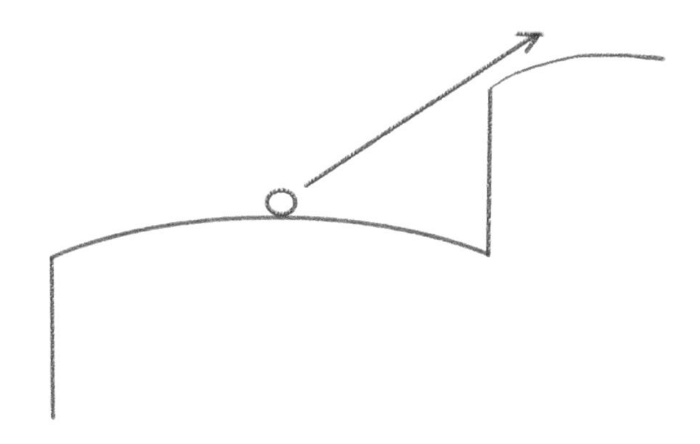

MOTIVATION: WHY WE PURSUE THE NEXT PLATEAU

Your pursuit of growth is deeply rooted in human nature. It is an innate drive that propels you forward toward the next plateau. Motivation comes from pursuing a vision of a bigger future. That future, which awaits on the next plateau, gives your journey purpose. Motivation is the energy that drives your jump.

In his popular book, *Drive: The Surprising Truth About What Motivates Us*, Daniel Pink expertly argues that traditional extrinsic or external forms of motivation are not as effective as intrinsic motivation in driving long-term, high-quality performance.[30]

In this context, motivations can be categorized into three distinct types: external, internal, and intrinsic. The following are my own definitions of these.

External Motivation: Pressure from Outside

This first category is fueled by external factors and incentives. These can include rewards such as grades, money, praise, or societal expectations. Understanding external motivation is important as it provides us with clear targets, benchmarks, and extrinsic rewards that can drive our actions and facilitate goal attainment.

However, relying solely on external motivation has potential drawbacks. Overt dependence on external rewards may lead you to lose sight of your intrinsic desires and personal growth. When the external incentives diminish or cease to exist, your motivation may wane, resulting in a lack of sustained effort and fulfillment.

In the Campground phase of a plateau, you experience success and positive feedback. However, you may begin to feel the gentle push of external pressure rather than internal motivation telling you to change. This can lead to a feeling of being stuck.

A study conducted at the University of Chicago demonstrates this phenomenon.[31] Researchers conducted a series of experiments in which participants completed a task and received positive feedback. In one experiment, participants were then given the option to continue working on the same task or switch to a new one. They found that those who felt *external* pressure to switch were *less* likely to continue working on the same task, even if they were enjoying it and felt they were making progress.

Interestingly, they also found that external pressure to switch to a new task reduced the amount of gratitude people felt in pursuing the current one, and it also increased the person's regret for not changing tasks sooner.[32]

These results indicate that external pressures not only hinder you from making the most impactful and long-lasting changes you need, but they steal your gratitude as well. Be on the alert for them. They exist everywhere, especially at the Canyon Wall.

Internal Motivation: Purpose from Inside

Internal motivation arises from within and is rooted in your personal goals, values, and aspirations. It comes from a sense of purpose, personal growth, and the desire for self-improvement.

Recognizing and harnessing internal motivations is vital for achieving meaningful change. It allows you to tap into your authentic desires and pursue personally meaningful goals. Internal motivations align with your values, providing you with a deep sense of fulfillment and intrinsic satisfaction when you achieve those goals.

However, be mindful of potential drawbacks. You may feel pressured to meet self-imposed expectations or forced to constantly re-evaluate yourself, either of which can lead to stress or burnout.

Intrinsic Motivation: Doing for Enjoyment's Sake

Nancy and Harry's values were a starting point in understanding what would motivate them to make the changes they needed to make, but those internal motivations weren't the only aspect. The third category, intrinsic motivation, represents the rest of the picture: the innate desires and enjoyment derived from engaging in an activity for its own sake. Here, you don't need external motivations; you're doing it for the love of it. Intrinsic motivation is driven by a genuine interest, curiosity, and passion for the activity itself. It fuels deep engagement, perseverance, and continuous improvement.

Intrinsic motivation allows you to experience a sense of joy, creativity, and just "being in the zone" during the pursuit of an activity. You may find that this type of motivation overlaps with your natural instincts as well. Recognizing and nurturing your intrinsic motivation is vital as you seek fulfillment on your next plateau.

When I asked Nancy and Harry what was important to them about their wealth, I wanted to get at the intrinsic motivations around the purpose for which that wealth existed. Once you begin to align your next plateau to your own intrinsic motivations, your purpose becomes clear, and your motivations become more enduring as they pursue more lasting significance.

ALIGNING MOTIVATION AND PURPOSE

Finding your next plateau requires that key ingredient of intrinsic motivation, but also something else.

Years ago, I was invited to speak to a group of financial advisors in Tokyo. While I was there, I became aware of a Japanese word, "ikigai." Ikigai is a compound word composed of "iki," which means "life," and "gai," which means "value" or "worth." Together, "ikigai" can be translated as "a reason for being" or "a sense of purpose in life." It refers to the intersection of four elements: what you love (intrinsic motivations), what you are uniquely good at (abilities), what the world needs (demand), and what you can be paid for providing (economic value).

Finding your ikigai is believed to bring satisfaction, fulfillment, and a sense of meaning to your life. Passion alone is not enough. You need to be good at what you strive to achieve, which takes time and effort. There also must be a demand for what you can provide, and, of course, in a business setting, people need to be willing to pay for it. (The latter may not be a requirement if this is a personal rather than a business jump.)

MINDSETS AS MOTIVATION

It is not enough to achieve a goal. What we seek is a state of mind that tells us we've done something positive.

Positive mindsets are actually motivating in their own right. To understand what I mean, let's look at the power of three different states of mind that fuel our journey in positive ways: gratitude, satisfaction, and happiness.

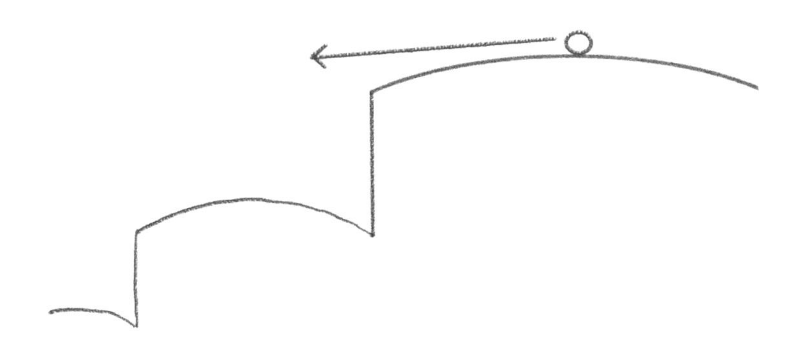

Gratitude: The Power of Looking Back

When I was growing up, each year, we would spend Christmas with my cousins at my Aunt Chi Chi's and Uncle Don's house in Dallas.

It was a wonderful older home built in the forties and remodeled over the years to their unique tastes. One thing they did not change, however, was a small hall bathroom. It was near the family room where we gathered to open presents each year, and my cousins and I would duck into that bathroom to check out the inside doorjamb, on which tiny pencil marks alongside dates and names noted our heights and the passage of time as we grew.

It was fun to gather around and look at how much each person had grown in a year. We could see how someone had hit a growth spurt one year, while in other years, there would barely be a change. Without fail, we would also compare the earliest mark on the doorjamb for that person to see how much they had grown since the beginning of recorded history (as far as we were concerned).

Not present on the doorjamb were any national statistics about where someone should have been compared to their peers or where they were expected to be by next year to measure up, so to speak. All that was present was where we were now and where we had been.

That's all we needed to have gratitude and energy. We had an inherent appreciation for what had occurred over time and for where we had come from.

As we inevitably find ourselves on a plateau, it's important that before we start seeking another plateau, we stop and appreciate where we have come from. There is science behind the gratitude philosophy. A focus on gratitude can provide more mental energy and motivation to make positive changes in our lives. When we are grateful for what we have, we are more likely to approach challenges and opportunities with a positive mindset and a sense of optimism.[33]

One way that gratitude can increase mental energy is by enhancing our overall sense of well-being. People who practice gratitude have higher levels of life satisfaction, positive affect, and resilience to stress. When you feel good about yourself and your life, you're more likely to have the mental energy and motivation to pursue goals and make positive changes. Making the next Plateau Jump becomes easier.

Think about it this way. Focusing your attention on one end of an emotional spectrum prevents the opposite end from gaining hold. The opposite of gratitude is not ingratitude but resentment. It's not a far slide from resentment into bitterness. Bitterness simply makes hard times worse. How many bitter people do you know who are making successful Plateau Jumps? If you say zero, you win the prize.

Satisfaction: The Rolling Stones Had It Wrong

When Mick Jagger sang about not getting any satisfaction, maybe it was because he was looking for it in the wrong place. Jagger may want to look at how plateauing can lead to the very thing he can't seem to get.

Someone like you who would read this book is someone striving for success and progress. Before you read the previous chapters in this book, the idea of reaching a plateau in your personal life or career may have seemed like a negative outcome. If I haven't yet convinced you that that perspective is incorrect, here's some additional evidence.

Researchers in Finland examined hundreds of employees, investigating the effects of job demands and job resources on work engagement and job satisfaction. The study focused on those who had experienced a short break or plateau in their work tasks. They found those who had experienced a plateau had higher levels of work engagement and job satisfaction compared to those who had not.[34]

The researchers suggested that experiencing a plateau may lead employees to focus on personal growth and development. In turn, that personal growth and development enhance their work engagement and job satisfaction. This means that, instead of viewing a plateau as a negative outcome, viewing it as an opportunity for growth and development can enable one to use it to improve one's life.

Interestingly, studies on adult development indicate that individuals often report higher satisfaction after going through significant life transitions or Plateau Jumps that involve personal growth. These studies suggest that even though the growth process can be challenging, the outcomes are typically positive in terms of life satisfaction.[35] Merely the pursuit of growth-oriented goals that align with an individual's personal values leads to higher levels of well-being and satisfaction over time.[36] Plateau Jumping is where you find satisfaction.

Satisfaction comes from making the most of opportunity, and opportunity occurs at plateaus. But it is only an opportunity open to those with the right mindset.

HAPPINESS: JEFFERSON HAD IT RIGHT

Thomas Jefferson had it right when he penned the Declaration of Independence: "We hold these truths to be self-evident, that all men are created equal, that they are endowed by their Creator with certain unalienable rights, that among these are Life, Liberty, and the pursuit of Happiness."[37]

Why didn't he just say we had the right to happiness? Why put the qualifier "the pursuit of" in front of happiness?

Jefferson understood that we are built for the *pursuit*. Not the immediacy of short-term pleasure-seeking but the seeking of a higher state of being.

This means not that we can never find the happiness we pursue but that once we find it, we are changed. We are genuinely happy. We then realize there can be more significance that makes us happier still — with a new happiness we could not have visualized until then. And so, a new pursuit ensues.

The very nature of human design is built around the necessity of our pursuit. Contentment would lead to our very demise as we would fail to do the things that help us survive. The seeking, the exploration, the growing.

Think about it. The things that made you happy as a child are not the things that make you happy later in life. Let's hope not. The things that made you happy ten years ago are not the things that will make you happy ten years from now. You will grow. As you grow, however you define happiness — whether as a calming sense or a heightened state — your anticipation of it is what causes you to seek the next plateau.

That is not to say that the happiness you previously felt wasn't real. It was. It is also not to say that you cannot be

THE THINGS THAT
MADE YOU HAPPY
TEN YEARS AGO ARE
NOT THE THINGS
THAT WILL MAKE YOU
HAPPY TEN YEARS
FROM NOW. YOU
WILL GROW.

happy where you are. You can. It turns out that it all starts with how we are defining the term.

What Kind of Happiness Do You Seek?

The term happiness can have two quite different meanings.

Hedonic Happiness – Hedonic ("pleasure") happiness focuses on activities that result in momentary pleasure. These activities are inward-focused and fleeting. While not bad in their own rights, the single-minded pursuit of this self-gratification would be damaging.

First, the happiness that is simply satisfying the proclivities of the present requires more of the same activity to maintain the initial feeling. The more you have, the more you want. Social comparisons add more pressure. We look at what others have and hedonistically decide we need it to make us happy.

Eudaimonic Happiness – In contrast, eudaimonic ("eu" meaning good or well, and "daimon" meaning guiding spirit or soul) happiness comes from activities that bring an overall feeling of accomplishment, one that comes from a life well lived. The term comes from what Aristotle described as the "pursuit of virtue, excellence, and the best within us." Eudaimonia is best translated as human flourishing or blessedness. It is the *pursuit* of virtue. Aristotle used the term as the highest form of good. The sum of a life well lived would be a higher form of happiness. That is what we are meant to pursue.

I don't think there is any doubt about which type Jefferson intended. Hedonic happiness was not what Jefferson had in mind. I believe he meant the pursuit of something more meaningful. A country of citizens living lives they can look back upon with satisfaction, feeling they were well lived in service to others, is no doubt superior to a country populated by inhabitants merely seeking momentary pleasure.

In addition, these two types of happiness are often in conflict. You give up a lot of short-term, hedonic pursuits to achieve the long-term eudaimonia that exists at the next plateau. It is that self-sacrifice of the former for the latter that puts us on the path to making the Plateau Jump. It is not the pursuit of happiness itself that is important, but the pursuit of those things that will result in happiness that matters. Be happy (or content) with what you have, but constantly pursue a worthy plateau.

Happiness Creates Success

This may seem counterintuitive, but your success in reaching the next plateau is not what will result in happiness. In fact, it is the other way around. Start with happiness, and success will follow.

OUR NATURAL MOTIVATION: GROWTH

As humans, we are all wired for growth. Within the depths of your being, there exists a natural inclination to learn, explore, and expand your horizons. This innate desire for growth and improvement is embedded in your brain, urging you to seek out new experiences and challenges that stretch your capabilities.

IT IS NOT THE PURSUIT
OF HAPPINESS ITSELF
THAT IS IMPORTANT,
BUT THE PURSUIT
OF THOSE THINGS
THAT WILL RESULT
IN HAPPINESS
THAT MATTERS.

We are seekers. At the core of our existence, we yearn for a sense of fulfillment, purpose, and contentment. Pursuit of a bigger future necessitates growth and change as we strive to improve ourselves and our circumstances. When that vision of the next plateau eclipses your fears, you can't help but jump toward it.

This searching brings opportunities to increase your competence and autonomy, pulling you forward, away from potential stagnation. It helps you avoid getting stuck in redundant and unfulfilling activities for too long. Some ways this natural motivation manifests are through curiosity, connectedness, and creativity.

Curiosity

Your brain is wired to crave novelty. You're naturally inclined to seek out new experiences and stimuli in the world around you, continuously expanding your perspectives and enriching your life.

When we're curious, we're drawn to explore, learn, and appreciate the wonders of the world. Walt Disney captured it well when he said, "We keep moving forward, opening new doors, and doing new things because we're curious, and curiosity keeps leading us down new paths."

Research in positive psychology supports the idea. Studies looked at intentionally cultivating traits like curiosity and its impact on well-being.[38] And guess what? Those who developed curiosity reported increased life satisfaction and overall well-being.

Curiosity opens doors to progress and opportunities. When you're curious, you embrace change and approach life with a positive and open mindset. It fuels the desire to take risks, learn from experiences, and find joy in exploring the possibilities of the next plateau.

Connectedness

We are social creatures by nature. Human beings thrive on connection and belonging, seeking meaningful relationships and interactions with others. Take a moment to notice, and you'll see a strong association between people's happiness and their relationships with family, friends, and community.

Most people want to ascend social hierarchies and gain recognition and belongingness. People naturally build these social hierarchies, and we naturally seek to climb them, or at least not fall down a rung. Many times, this desire pushes us to gain competencies that are tied to social validation, acceptance, and an ongoing quest for esteem.

Pursuing growth and change within our social sphere opens avenues for us to build new relationships, expand our social networks, and find novel ways to connect with like-minded individuals who share our aspirations and values. These relationships can, in turn, support our growth in other areas as we gain knowledge and assistance from others in our networks.

Creativity

If you fail to fuel motivation with the clear purpose of a compelling plateau, that motivation wanes, and the possibilities of a bigger future diminish. Pablo Picasso said, "All children are artists. The problem is how to remain an artist once we grow up."

Picasso knew we changed over time and that our uncultivated strengths would atrophy. This is supported by authors George Ainsworth-Land and Beth Jarman in their book *Breakpoint and Beyond: Mastering the Future Today.* In it, they cite a study on creativity that Land conducted in 1968. Land took one of NASA's creativity tests used with innovative engineers and administered it to 1,600 five-year-olds. In the results, 98 percent of the children rated genius level on creativity. By age 10, only 30 percent of the group rated at this same level, and by age 15, that number had dropped to only 12 percent. When 280,000 adults took the same creativity test, the number dropped to 2 percent.[39]

As many people grow older, they tend to settle into what they know rather than seek what they do not know. They stop looking for the next plateau. They stop even trying to think about it. That's unfortunate because creativity — particularly visualization — is crucial to finding your next plateau.

You may be familiar with the famous marshmallow test performed by Walter Mischel in 1972 at Stanford.[40] The study spanned some thirty years. It is included in many books about human motivation and the importance of impulse control.

The researchers would place a marshmallow in front of a six-year-old and then leave the room. The child was told that when the researcher returned at some undetermined time, they could have another marshmallow if they would just wait until then to eat the first one. The bargain was to resist the impulse to eat the first one and be rewarded with a second!

What the researchers were studying was how the children dealt with delayed gratification. Some punted on the whole idea of waiting and ate the marshmallow right away, forfeiting the potential second one. Others used distraction techniques like singing or looking away from the marshmallow so they could endure the agony of delayed gratification in exchange for their second marshmallow reward.

Here is where it gets interesting. At one point, they placed the second marshmallow along with the first on the table in front of the child. The instructions were simply to wait to eat the two marshmallows. As would be expected, the results changed a little when they had no additional incentive to wait. Impulse control got worse with the second "reward" marshmallow staring them in the face. Overall, the children found it harder to resist when the rewards were visible. Ok, not a big surprise. More people go for the temptation if it's staring them right in the face, and there's no downside to not waiting.

But then the researchers did something else. They replaced the second "reward" marshmallow on the table with *just a photograph* of the second marshmallow, with the instructions going back to the same as the first part of the study: Wait to eat the first marshmallow, and you'll get the second "reward" one, too. Here's the thing: The photo got the same result as having a real marshmallow there. The subjects of the experiment still couldn't hold out as long. Their brains considered the photograph — a visualization — to be the same thing as a real marshmallow.

This is how your brain sees your visualization of the next plateau — as real. The more you visualize it, the more it will motivate you.

By the way, the research team tracked the children over time and found that those with the greatest impulse control and the ability to delay immediate gratification for a future reward ended up performing better socially and academically later in life. That's probably not a big surprise. It illustrates that no matter how motivating something is, you still must have discipline in pursuing it. Jump to that next higher plateau too soon and without preparation, and you'll get altitude sickness.

The key takeaway is that you can visualize your own next plateau, and the impact on your behavior will be the same as seeing it. For you, it's already real. Visualizing your next plateau can be as impactful as witnessing it firsthand. In your mind's eye, it's already a reality. This can result in your becoming complacent, feeling like you've achieved it (yet being constantly disappointed in some way you can't explain), or it can result in your being inspired to achieve it.

In the second option, the vision you've conjured is vivid and palpable, far from a mere illusion. Striving for a mere mirage of a vision would be like chasing the wind. When you not only have the vision but believe achieving it is worth doing — when it's aligned with your values and your true motivation — you will go on to achieve it. In the ensuing chapters, we'll delve into strategies to bring your vision to fruition more effectively.

What are my core values?

How well do I acknowledge and show gratitude for the progress I have made on my personal journey?

Am I living a life in a way that happiness will be the result?

What are my intrinsic motivations for seeking the next plateau?

Am I keeping a clear perspective?

What actions can I take to move to a state of better stress?

SECTION 2

MASTERING MOVEMENT: Five Levers of Change

When embarking on the journey of Plateau Jumping, you'll naturally start searching for the tools that can help make your desired change happen. Multiple books have been written on each of the five levers of change discussed here. What I've included is brief. The good news is, you don't need to pull all those levers at once — and some, maybe not at all. It's about figuring out which ones are right for you. Once you read this, you may think of a few more ideas about how to use the levers on your own. But these guidelines should get you started in the right direction.

CHAPTER 5

Plateau Systems

SIMPLICITY JUMPS COMPLEXITY

"It's not about perfect. It's about effort. And when you bring that effort every single day, that's where transformation happens. That's how change occurs."
— JILLIAN MICHAELS, FITNESS TRAINER

"The first step towards getting somewhere is to decide you're not going to stay where you are." — J.P. MORGAN, AMERICAN FINANCIER

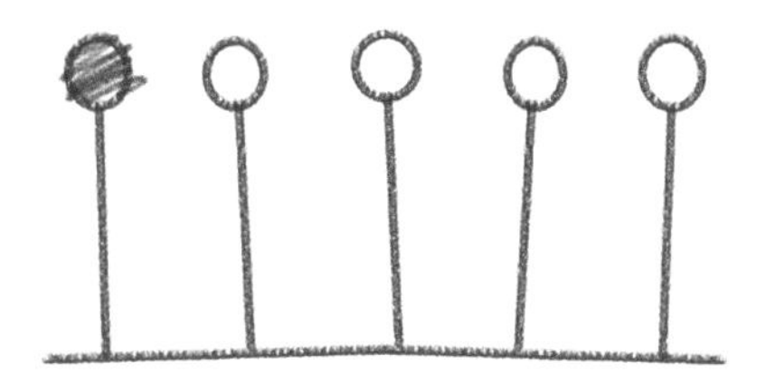

SYSTEMS ARE "THE WAY"

THE PACKING LIST was next to me as I prepared for the Camino de Santiago. El Camino means "the way" in Spanish, and I was preparing to walk the path, thus named for Santiago

— St. James the Great. My journey would take me from Saint Jean Pied de Port, France, to Santiago de Compostela, Spain. It would take me about thirty days to cover the 500-mile pilgrimage.

The Camino de Santiago has been traveled by hundreds of thousands of pilgrims for over a thousand years. I was about to join those who had sought solace, spiritual awakening, and personal transformation along this same path.

Established after the liberation of Granada in 1492 and declared by Pope Alexander VI to be one of the three great pilgrimages in Christendom, it follows, in some parts, roads and bridges built by the Romans. Most of it is simply a solitary path through the Spanish countryside. It reaches out to touch the small villages and towns where it draws near and then continues shepherding its pilgrims all the way to the cathedral in Santiago de Compostela. The Cathedral of Santiago is where it is said the relics of Saint James are kept. It is the place the trail takes you, but the journey may take you somewhere different.

For some, the pilgrimage is a religious experience trusting in God to provide for safe passage and stopping at the chapels and cathedrals along the way to worship and pray. For others, it is an athletic adventure to test themselves by covering the span of Spain with nothing but what they can carry on their backs. For me, it was a little of both; it was my next plateau.

Reality Demands a New Plan

I walked this journey of faith and exploration during one summer when I took some time away from the office. I was still years away from selling my business but no less interested in seeking a new plateau.

My plan was to walk across the northern part of Spain and culminate the experience with the Catholic mass at the Cathedral of Santiago. I eagerly awaited the experience of watching as the massive *botafumerio*, the censer in which holy incense is burned, would swing across the Cathedral's nave and billow its smoke from the ornate encasement while the priest blessed us all in a mix of Spanish and Latin.

As with any jump to a new plateau, I wasn't entirely certain what I would experience once I arrived. To prepare, I trained and read all I could get my hands on for months in advance. I developed a training system to hike a specific number of miles per day and taper off as the departure day approached. This way, I could avoid the risk of injury close to the hike.

Trial and error became my teacher as I learned what to pack and what not to pack. I developed a system that provided easy access to rain gear should the need suddenly arise. I evenly distributed the weight of my pack by placing the heavier items near the middle for comfort and balance.

A hydration system was integrated into the backpack, with a small tube from which I could drink water and not stop walking. I had practiced all of this at home in Texas, logging hundreds of miles with my gear strapped to my back. Slowly hiking along the trail that followed the Trinity River near my home, I honed my hiking systems.

So I thought.

But it only took me a week on the Camino de Santiago to realize that plans and reality can diverge. I got tired earlier in the day than I expected. I was hiking twenty or so miles a day, but it felt like more. I was struggling to keep pace with the plan I had made. I was dragging.

Just outside of Pamplona, Spain, I stopped at a small town and found the local post office. As the residents of this small Spanish village went about their day walking past me, I dumped everything from my pack onto the sidewalk. Whatever system I thought I had perfected, it needed changing.

I sorted everything into two piles: things I absolutely needed to be able to continue the Camino and things that I did not. Into the first pile went my socks, shorts, T-shirt, and glasses. Only the basics. In the other pile, I put the extra hat, a collapsible cup, a small collapsible chair, and a book I thought I would read. The pile of nonessentials was embarrassingly large.

Left with little more than two pairs of clothes, a headlamp, and the shoes on my feet, I boxed up everything in the nonessentials pile and mailed it home. Good riddance.

I had discovered essentialism. There were things I just didn't need. Our systems only need to be as robust as necessary and no more. My burden was now lighter.

If I was going to finish this journey, my systems needed to change. I didn't need more equipment to make the journey; I needed less. I needed simplicity.

Days later, I approached the Cruz de Ferro along the Camino's path. The Cruz de Ferro (Iron Cross) is a tall cross that sits atop a sprawling pile of small rocks contributed over the decades by pilgrims walking the Camino. It is common for a pilgrim to bring a small rock from home, tossing it over their shoulder onto the pile as a symbolic act of letting go of their inner burdens.

I took a deep breath as I stood for a long time in front of the cross and its attending stones, left by pilgrims who had

OUR SYSTEMS
ONLY NEED TO
BE AS ROBUST AS
NECESSARY AND
NO MORE.

come before me. I dug deep into my pack of essentials and found the stone I had brought from home. Just a rock with seemingly no real function, it had nevertheless been in my "essential" pile on the sidewalk in front of the post office near Pamplona. Its journey was ending here. I felt the weight of the stone and the burdens, doubts, and fears — more nonessentials — slip from my fingers as I tossed it toward the base of the cross. It was impossible not to recognize that I should also cast not just the stone but also all my cares upon the enduring symbol of ultimate sacrifice and redemption.

One hundred and forty miles later, I arrived early at Santiago as the city was waking up. As I stood in front of the Cathedral de Santiago thirty days and five hundred miles after I began, I had a strange feeling.

I had expected to feel relief and satisfaction that the ordeal was over or perhaps a feeling of completion for having accomplished the pilgrimage. The feeling you get crossing the finish line of a marathon. Instead, I felt this tugging at my core to continue. I wanted to keep walking. To keep the journey of growth alive. There were lessons to take home but more yet to learn. I returned home, but I brought the journey and its lessons with me, continuing them in a different way.

Applying the New Lessons

When I arrived back at the office in Texas, I used what I had learned on the trail and began to streamline my systems. It was time to get rid of more nonessentials.

I tossed out many of the unnecessarily complex business-management systems I had built years before and replaced them with stripped-down approaches that not only reduced complexity and expenses but also produced better results. The investment models became simpler and more efficient. I eliminated some of the services we said we provided but had never been exceptionally good at. We became clearer about what our core services were, and with this focus, we became excellent. I reduced our client base where the fit wasn't right and helped some of our clients find better relationships that met their needs.

Redundant reporting systems that had weighed down our operations were eliminated. Gone were all the endless spreadsheets with recalculations of the same meaningless numbers. Instead, I found one important number to track: the number of meetings with clients. If our primary role was to build long-term relationships with our clients, everything would be built from that measure. As we boiled our tracking down to this one thing, this one thing improved. It drove new business, greater client satisfaction, and new referrals. A sign that we were doing something right!

The purpose of reducing the systems in your life is not merely to focus on what remains but to eliminate the energy consumption associated with increased decision-making. If you can eliminate the nonessentials, you will free up the time and energy associated with them and devote it to more essential activities.

GET RID OF THE STUFF

When attempting to organize my office to eliminate redundant systems and get to the essentials, I started thinking of how to organize my desk supplies, files, in-basket, work-in-process, etc. However, visits to the office supply store to buy containers and organizational gadgets didn't seem to sit right. Something was off.

Then I realized why: I was falling into another trap. This approach was just moving the stuff around, but it was essentially still in the backpack. Shifting it from one pocket to the other wasn't going to help ease the weight.

Instead, what about getting rid of the stuff, like I did on the sidewalk in Spain?

There is a story from the creation of the great statue of *David*, which many consider the greatest work of sculpture ever crafted. When asked about how he was able to create such a brilliant sculpture, Michelangelo responded that *David* was already inside the stone. All Michelangelo needed to do was to slowly chip away and reveal the magnificent sculpture that was there all along, underneath all that extra stone.

All of my stuff was like that extra stone. What was underneath?

I got rid of the office desk with all its drawers and replaced it with the black granite conference table. No drawers, no stuff. I took the trash can out of my office. No trash can, no trash. I moved out the file cabinets and shifted to electronic files. No office supplies, no in-basket, nothing but the essentials I needed to meet with a client. A place to sit and talk. That's it.

I had been dealing with the clutter by trying to organize all my stuff when the cause of the clutter and chaos was that there was stuff to begin with. After chipping away at all of that, my focus was now on my primary role, meeting with and listening to my clients, unencumbered by distractions that competed for my focus. The only systems I kept were those supporting that role.

Make Predetermined Decisions

Taking a cue from Albert Einstein, Steve Jobs, Mark Zuckerberg, and others, my wardrobe became simpler. Though not as extreme as those guys, I bought nothing but white shirts or blue shirts and eliminated the clutter and chaos of figuring out what to wear.

Once you decide what you are going to do to reach your next plateau, making decisions becomes easier. Saying no to things that don't take you to the next plateau seems difficult at first. It gets easier with clarity of purpose.

I know business owners who don't take breakfast meetings because that's when they are at their most creative for writing content. There are people who turn down lunch requests on Fridays because that's when they have lunch with their spouses and kids. A business-owner friend of mine turns down invitations to fancy dinners and conferences from vendors because he decided long ago to keep his analysis of suppliers unencumbered by any feelings of reciprocity for "gifts" he might receive. Deciding ahead of time reduces the energy burned by making those misaligned decisions each time and keeps you focused on the next jump.

SYSTEMS ACTIONS

Following are some actions you can take to streamline your own systems.

1. **Conduct a systems audit:** Take the time to thoroughly assess your existing systems and routines across various areas of your life, such as work, relationships, health, and personal development.

2. **Lighten your pack:** Eliminate the systems or processes that are weighing you down. Keep what works, adjust what doesn't, and be open to adapting and refining your approach as you learn and grow.

3. **Decide in advance:** Look for opportunities to make a singular decision that will eliminate other decisions.

4. **Find your one thing:** Discover your "one thing" nearest the cause of what you are trying to impact, and focus on that.

In the movie *City Slickers*[41], Billy Crystal's character asks the wise old cowboy, Curly, about the meaning of life.

Curly stops his horse and turns to Crystal. "The meaning of life," he says, "is this one thing." He holds up one finger and pauses.

"What? What is it?" Crystal asks.

Pointing that finger at Crystal, Curly replies, "That's what you have to figure out."

That breaks the focus down to the essential point. Know that, and you build your systems of life around that. Know that, and you say no to things that pull you away from it.

PLATEAU-JUMPING QUESTIONS

What systems am I successfully using at my current plateau?

What systems should travel with me to my next plateau? What systems should I leave behind?

What nonessential commitments should I be saying no to?

What tasks or responsibilities can I delegate or outsource to others to free up more time for my essential pursuits?

Are there any outdated or ineffective systems I'm holding onto? How can I identify and let go of these systems to create space for new possibilities?

How can I establish predetermined decisions or guidelines to reduce decision-making and simplify my life?

CHAPTER 6

Plateau Habits

EASE JUMPS FRICTION

"The chains of habit are too weak to be felt until they are too strong to be broken."

— SAMUEL JOHNSON, AUTHOR

"We are what we repeatedly do. Excellence, then, is not an act but a habit."

— ARISTOTLE, PHILOSOPHER

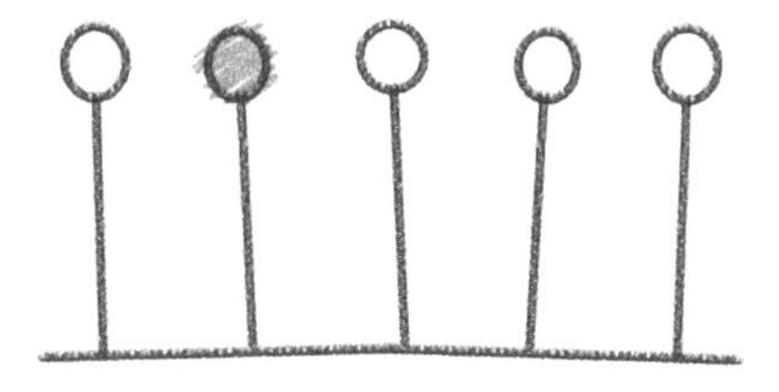

I STOOD AT the summit of Mount Kilimanjaro, looking down on the glaciers and beyond the clouds below. It had been a different journey entirely from my experience at Mount Everest base camp — I had avoided altitude sickness this time.

It was 2023 when my wife Melissa and I summited the Tanzanian mountain. Kilimanjaro is the highest point in Africa, standing at an elevation of 19,341 feet. It is a tough, multi-day trek that forces you to slowly acclimate to the ever-diminishing oxygen levels as you ascend higher and higher.

As you move higher, your adrenaline, drive, and culture push you to hurry up the mountain while the guides and porters repeatedly say a phrase to remind you to do just the opposite. "*Polé, polé,*" they will say to you in Swahili. It means "slowly, slowly," and it is so habitual as to almost be a greeting. Scrambling past you on the rocky trail, carrying their oversized loads, porters will automatically say, "*polé, polé.*" Slowly, slowly.

"The summit will be there," the guides will remind you. "Go *polé, polé*, and you will be at the summit soon enough."

What they know is what I learned the hard way on the Tibetan Plateau — that if you overexert yourself and ascend too quickly, the altitude will win. The days before you summit, you are at altitudes higher than any point in the lower forty-eight states. If you rush, you will exhaust yourself, or worse, altitude sickness will set in as it did for me in Tibet. If that happens, the guides will bring you down. Your quest will end.

Determined not to make the mistake I did in Tibet, I followed the habitual advice. Slowly, slowly, I followed our guide and placed one foot ever so slowly, slowly in front of the other. After a while, it started to become a habit.

We left the relative warmth of our sleeping bags inside our tents at 3:00 a.m. on summit day to begin what would be a long day's climb to the top. The bitterly cold air made me shiver and shook away the last memories of what little sleep I had gotten. I had no trouble remembering to maintain my new habit. The bitter cold had left a frost over everything, and everyone was moving slowly. As usual, my natural drive made me want to hurry. "Let's get up there!" However, I stayed mindful of the habits the guides had established, which would serve us well and cause us to follow the proper process of pacing ourselves.

Eleven hours later, as we summited, I was thankful for the advice. Going slowly fought against my instinct to hurry up and make the climb. If I could change my habit of rushing, what other habits could I change? What habits did I need to change? That all depended on what challenge I wanted to climb next.

CREATE KEYSTONE HABITS

In his book, *The Power of Habit,* Charles Duhigg refers to the term "keystone habits."[42] Keystone habits are those habits that automatically lead to multiple positive behaviors and positive effects in your life.

Take a moment to think about your habits and identify those that have the most significant impact on your desired outcomes. There are many great examples of keystone habits. For example, maintaining a daily journal might serve as a keystone habit leading to improved self-awareness, mindfulness, and goal-setting.

Daily exercise is also a keystone habit, emphasizing its positive impact on physical and mental well-being. Engaging in regular exercise can trigger a chain reaction of positive changes, including healthier eating habits, improved self-discipline, and increased self-confidence.

The habit of making your bed in the morning is a keystone habit. It creates a sense of order and discipline that can spill over into other areas of life, such as work, relationships, and personal organization.

Another example would be family dinners. Families who regularly gather for meals tend to have better communication, stronger relationships, and healthier eating habits. The simple act of having regular family dinners can create a positive domino effect on various aspects of family life.

FRICTION INFLUENCES HABITS

In 2022, Sanger and I spoke with behavioral scientist Wendy Wood on the *Decidedly* podcast.[43] Professor Wood has conducted extensive research on habit formation and the impact of environmental cues on behavior. She has explored topics such as the influence of contextual cues on habit performance, and the interplay between habits and conscious decision-making.

In our discussion, we talked about how to create positive habits and also how to use habits to aid decision-making.

Use Friction to Influence Good Habits

Habits are automatic actions triggered by associated contextual cues. For example, we fasten our seatbelts upon entering a car. We check the rearview mirror before driving. Extensive psychological research shows that when we repeat a simple action in a consistent context, it activates whenever we are exposed to that context. We form habits through associative learning.

In this way, society has harnessed the power of contextual cues to create positive change. One example is in the campaign against drunk driving.

In the early 1980s, the United States faced a significant challenge with alcohol-related driving fatalities and crashes due to driving under the influence (DUI). In 1985, of the 43,825 fatal automobile crashes in the U.S., 41 percent (18,125) of were alcohol related, as per the Insurance Information Institute.[44]

The prevalence of this dangerous habit demanded action. As a society, we began to place *friction* in front of this habit. Advertisements and messages highlighting the potential consequences of driving under the influence are strategically placed in locations associated with alcohol consumption, such as bars and restaurants. These messages, associated with the context of drinking establishments, effectively serve as reminders to patrons to make responsible decisions and find alternative transportation if they have been drinking.

The implementation of friction-inducing measures has played a crucial role in reducing both the percentage and absolute number of alcohol-related fatalities. In addition to the messaging, stricter enforcement efforts, such as sobriety checkpoints and random breathalyzer tests, have made it increasingly difficult and socially unacceptable for individuals to drive under the influence.

These measures have led to a significant decline in alcohol-related fatalities over the years. By 2021, though there were around the same total number of fatal accidents, total the alcohol-related fatalities dropped to only 31 percent of that, at 13,384.[45] There is work still to do, but friction is playing a part in making a change in behavioral habits.

Just as in climbing Kilimanjaro, the change we create through a change in habits will happen *polé, polé*, and through that determination, any habit we have can be reshaped. Our habits become who we are. They morph into our character. That character becomes our future at the next plateau. If we can create the necessary habits to jump to the next plateau and eliminate the detrimental habits, our jump will be easier — just as my climb to the summit of Mount Kilimanjaro was easier than my climb to the base camp of Mount Everest.

Use Friction to Smoke Out a Bad Habit

It's important to create an environment that bolsters desired habits while deterring negative ones. Let's explore an example of how society successfully introduced friction to reduce another harmful habit.

One of the most influential coming-of-age movies of the 1960s was *The Graduate*.[46] In the 1967 movie, Dustin Hoffman portrays a recent college graduate making his own Plateau Jump in life. Hoffman's character, Benjamin Braddock, is depicted smoking to mimic the perceived sophistication of that activity at the time.

In 1960, nearly 42 percent of Americans were smokers, with cigarette smoking ingrained deeply in our societal fabric. However, a transformation has taken place over the course of several decades, leading to a significant decline in smoking rates.

The decline in smoking can be attributed to the implementation of various friction-inducing measures that have reshaped societal norms and behaviors. One friction-inducing

OUR HABITS

BECOME WHO

WE ARE.

factor has been the introduction of comprehensive tobacco control policies, including advertising restrictions, increased taxation on tobacco products, graphic warning labels on cigarette packaging, and the creation of smoke-free environments in public places. As crazy as it now seems, you could have watched *The Graduate* on a plane while smoking until 1990, when the US banned in-flight smoking entirely.

These measures disrupted the tobacco industry's ability to entice new smokers and effectively discouraged many existing smokers from continuing their habit. These laws not only curbed direct exposure to secondhand smoke but also shifted social norms, making smoking less socially acceptable.

Over the long term, these friction-inducing measures have yielded impressive results. By 2019, smoking rates in the United States had plummeted to approximately 13.7 percent, a drastic decline from the 42 percent reported in 1960.[47] This downward trajectory is a testament to the power of societal friction in reshaping habits and behaviors.

MAKE HABITS VISIBLE AND TANGIBLE

James Clear's *Atomic Habits*[48] emphasizes the importance of making habits visible and concrete. To reinforce the power of habits, define your new positive habits in specific and measurable terms. Instead of vaguely committing to "improving productivity," establish a clear habit of dedicating 30 minutes every morning to prioritize daily tasks.

Clear suggests creating a habit tracker, which is a visible and tangible tool to monitor and record your daily habits.

This could be a simple chart or a habit-tracking app that allows you to mark each day you successfully complete a habit. The act of visually tracking your habits provides a sense of accomplishment and helps you stay accountable.

STACK HABITS

Habit stacking, as coined by S.J. Scott in his book not coincidentally named *Habit Stacking,* involves linking a new habit to an existing one.[49] With this, you identify an established habit that you perform consistently, and then you pair it with a new habit you wish to cultivate.

For instance, if you already practice daily meditation, attach the habit of writing down three things you are grateful for immediately afterward. Or suppose you want to establish a habit of doing push-ups every morning. You could stack it with your habit of brushing your teeth: After brushing your teeth, you immediately do a set of push-ups.

By leveraging existing routines, you create natural triggers for your desired habits, facilitating long-term adherence.

HABITS ACTIONS

1. Decide on one new tangible habit you will need at your next plateau.

2. Now, think of a current habit — perhaps a keystone habit — that you could habit-stack your new one with to make it stick better. Pick a routine action such as

brushing your teeth, getting dressed, even feeding the dog — something you do every day. How can you attach the new habit to one of these routines?

3. Examine your current habits to see if any will interfere with your next plateau. For instance, on your next plateau, if you want to be fit and at optimal weight but you have a habit of just mindlessly eating in front of the TV, this habit will conflict with the plateau goal.

4. Determine a way to eliminate or change this conflicting habit. Look for ways to use friction to eliminate bad habits or encourage the formation of the desired new ones. For instance, you could take a walk instead of watching TV, or you could use a cycling machine in front of the TV rather than mindless snacking. An easy example to imagine is to add friction to a habit of grabbing junk food by making it difficult to access in your house. It's the old trick of putting the cookies on the top shelf. (Or, not buying them at all comes to mind.)

5. Create a system for tracking your success. You could track your progress in a phone app, post a checklist in a strategic location on your wall or whiteboard where you will see it, or just make a note on your calendar every day.

If you pay attention to the habits you cultivate, you can shape positive habits and break free from negative patterns. Whether it's leveraging keystone habits, making habits visible and tangible, habit stacking, or redesigning your environment, you have the tools to initiate lasting change. Creating habits will act as a catalyst, creating a ripple effect that influences other habits and behaviors. Changing habits can be a key lever to utilize when making your jump.

Remember, habit change is a gradual process, and it requires consistent effort and patience. But it's worth it. By taking these action steps and embracing the journey, you are setting yourself up for success in making substantive changes to your habits and transforming your life.

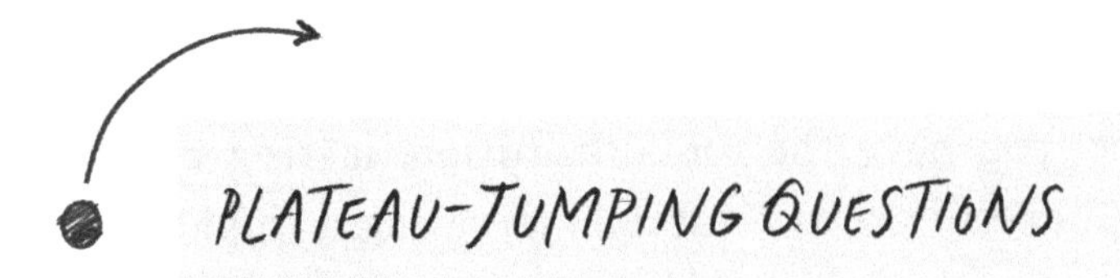

PLATEAU-JUMPING QUESTIONS

What habits do individuals who are already at the next plateau possess?

Which of your current habits support your well-being and goals, and which ones hinder your progress?

What values of yours are attached to the habits you will be creating?

CHAPTER 7

Plateau Goals

SPECIFICITY JUMPS VAGUENESS

"What you get by achieving your goals is not as important as what you become by achieving your goals." — ZIG ZIGLAR

"When you have a clear vision of your goal, it's easier to take the first step toward it." — L.L. BARKAT, AUTHOR

TAKING A "PEAK" AT GOAL-SETTING

MY FATHER AND I began our hike up Barr Trail to Pikes Peak early on a cool morning in September. As we started up the roughly 13-mile trail to the summit, the path was wide and smooth. I remember starting with a big jump onto the trail, landing on both feet and declaring the start of the hike.

The excursion would take us up to the top of the 14,110-foot mountain and back again. It was not normally a particularly challenging hike.

The first mile took about twenty minutes. At that rate, I calculated, we could be up and back, completing the 25.2-mile hike, by early that evening.

But things change.

After a few hours, at about 11:30 a.m., we reached Barr Camp, which sits at an elevation of 10,200 feet. We were now slightly off our 20-minute-per-mile pace. After a brief stop at the camp, we pressed on, desperate to get back on pace to complete the round-trip hike by nightfall. The next mile took an hour, and as the trail became steeper, our pace slowed.

Things were changing.

As my father and I stopped for another break, I calculated that with our current pace, we were unlikely to return by nightfall. With just under five miles to go to the summit, we could make the peak by 4:30 p.m., but there was little hope of making it back down the 12.6 miles in the dark.

This is when we swallowed our pride, and I used my cell phone to call my sister Stephanie.

Stephanie lives in Colorado Springs with her family. We had flown in the night before for a short visit. Unlike us, she had watched the weather forecast on the news the previous day. She had more than mildly suggested that today was a less-than-optimal day to be attempting a hike up to the peak. Hiking the day after you fly in from near seal level is another mistake.

Of course, we had totally disregarded her wise counsel.

Now that we had realized our mistake, she agreed to drive up to the road on the other side of the mountain to pick us up at the summit at 4:30 p.m. She did a respectable job of not giving us the "I told you so" speech.

But now, snow had gently started to fall. Things were about to change again.

The next leg of the hike was above the tree line. As a blanket of white began to cover the trail, the only way to ensure we were heading in the right direction was to keep our focus on the purpose of the hike — the summit. My focus became shorter. I measured my goals in feet. Getting to the next snow-covered rock outcropping became a small, achievable goal. I made sure each one kept us on a path to the summit.

As altitude sickness caused us to slow even more, I was taking more and longer rest stops. My head was pounding. Then I threw up.

I was wondering if I would make it at all, much less by when I had told Stephanie. I finally had to swallow my pride again and call Stephanie a second time.

"Can you make it 5:00 p.m. rather than 4:30 p.m.?" I asked sheepishly.

This time, there was no attempt to hold back. "It's snowing now! I told you so! You guys are idiots." she said with sort of a laugh in her voice.

"Be that as it may," I responded, "how about five o'clock?"

"I'll see you then." She hung up.

As we slowly made our way up the mountain, the snow worsened.

We drifted off the trail time and time again as it continued to become buried deeper by the blanket of snow. The trail, the way forward, was now obscured by the snow. The path was unclear, but the summit was visible. The summit was our goal. The only way to progress was to maintain a focus on the goal and work our way toward it. We continued to focus on the summit and on overcoming the obstacles presented by a now-invisible trail. We continued to slowly set small goals, which we even more slowly continued to meet.

At about 5:15 p.m., we arrived at the summit, tired, cold, and feeling the full effects of the altitude. The snow continued. However, now the real problem was that not only was Stephanie not there to meet us, no one was there.

Not a single person besides us was on top of the mountain. It was late, it was snowing, and we were the only people there. I searched for the cell phone in my pack and dialed her number again, praying that I would get a signal.

"Hello," she answered, with a tone of someone who expects your call.

"Hey, where are you?" I said, trying to sound upbeat.

"Well, they closed the road about an hour ago because of the snow."

"So... what do we do now?" I said, really hoping that some plan had been hatched when she found out the road was closed.

"I called the park service. They said you shouldn't have been up there in this weather and that basically you're hosed." Her statement was followed by a silence that had a ring of finality.

"That's comforting," I said sarcastically, then wished I hadn't been rude. "Dad is looking for a way to get inside the observation building up here," I told her. "I'll keep you posted."

As my father and I looked around the observation building for any way inside, we shook our heads and gave each

THE ONLY WAY
TO PROGRESS WAS
TO MAINTAIN A
FOCUS ON THE GOAL
AND WORK OUR
WAY TOWARD IT.

other the looks that said, "This is going to be a long, cold, uncomfortable night."

But things change.

We kept circling the building like people who have lost their keys and keep checking their pockets, hoping to find a different result. As my father and I came around the back side of the building for the third or fourth time, we heard a door open. What we didn't know is that the park service drops someone off at the Pikes Peak observation building each night as a security measure. The young man inside had heard us trying the doors and came out to see what was going on. Much to our relief, he allowed us to sleep inside the building that night.

As we woke up early the next morning, we were treated to a sight that few people in this world ever get to see: the sunrise view from the top of Pikes Peak. The beautiful glow slowly emerging over Colorado Springs was a sight that my father and I got to share. That was our reward.

Sometimes, you reach your goals by overcoming unexpected obstacles because things change. The path forward is not always discernable. In business and in life, we must keep our eye on the summit even when we lose our trail in the snow. Our rewards for pressing on are often greater than we imagined, and often, it is the journey that we value even more than the success of achieving the goal.

DEVELOP A PERSONAL PLAN

In my wealth management business, we had a process of meeting with each employee quarterly to discuss their

Personal Development Plan (PDP). The quarterly meeting was designed to help advance each employee toward their own personal Plateau Jump. Those who were of a growth mindset enjoyed it. If they were content in the Campground, however, it would get uncomfortable because the idea was to seek ways to grow.

I'll share the process we used because it is adaptable to any situation in which a person seeks growth, including your own.

Start with Vision and Values

Each quarter, we always started with the employee's personal values, which were written on the first page. We also included the company's values, but the employee's values were the guiding star. Next to their values, we wrote down their mission for their current role.

The first objective of the meeting was to gain clarity on what the employee wanted their role to develop into. Next, we looked at what they envisioned ahead, career-wise and personally. What did they want to happen?

We often talked about personal vision so their career aspirations could support their personal goals and vice versa. If they wanted to be able to spend more time coaching Little League or developing a hobby, we talked about it. Often, we could adjust work schedules or create flex-time arrangements to accommodate the personal goals.

This was our starting point for all the discussions. If you are planning a Plateau Jump, it is important to know what you envision. The next step is to turn the vagaries into specifics by setting clear goals.

Establish Short-Term Goals

Each quarter, we kept their bigger vision in mind and established short-term goals that would advance them toward their next plateau. These would be specific, attainable objectives we could measure within the next 90 days until we met again. These short-term goals supported what they wanted to see happen and were aligned with their personal values.

When establishing goals to align with someone's values, I have never had someone set a goal that contradicted their values. Remember back to the values discussion I had with Harry and Nancy? As in that, the challenge usually comes when someone's values do not have an outlet in their enumerated goals.

The conversation would go like this: "Hmm, learning is one of your values, but you don't seem to have mentioned a goal that would incorporate that value into what you plan to work on." We would then return to the list of projects for the quarter and work to ensure each value had an outlet.

If you have values that are not finding an outlet at your next plateau, take a moment to make certain you are pointed toward the right plateau. It is time to reassess those values. You can't jump very far if your values are misaligned with where you are claiming you want to go. Living in misalignment will slow your jump.

Doug Lennick is the founder of Think2Perform, a professional coaching and leadership consulting firm. When he joined us on the *Decidedly* podcast, he made the insightful observation that when we establish goals, they must first be put through an acid test. The acid test is asking ourselves, "Am I willing to do what it takes to achieve this goal?"[50]

Obviously, to answer Doug's question, you would have to know what it takes. You must know the cost of time and energy and be willing and able to pay that cost.

By being *willing*, you are aligning the goal with your motivations, and by being *able*, you are aligning your capabilities. Both of those factors need to be present to make certain you have an achievable short-term goal.

Establish the Plan

With our Plateau Jump established, we had a clearer understanding of what the employee wanted. We aligned this with their values, which provided motivation. Now, we had three to four items they could achieve within the next quarter that would move them along toward their career or personal development objectives.

Developing the plan to achieve the short-term goals means applying the "when," "who," and "how" to the goal. This would involve enlisting an accountability partner, scheduling time to work on the tasks required, and even setting up a checklist or process for monitoring progress. If the short-term goal is *what* you are going to do, the plan is the *when*, *who*, and *how*.

Perhaps you've heard of the study done at Harvard (or was it Yale?) that tracked graduates over time. The study showed that only 3 percent of the graduates had specific written goals before graduation. Twenty years later, it was shown that those graduates had earnings that were ten times those of the rest of their graduating class that had no clear goals. Obviously, there is something to setting goals and writing them down! Even if they are just short-term quarterly goals.

(Remember this study when we get to the chapter on Beliefs. We will revisit this.)

Take Action

Any process worth its salt eventually is reduced into action. We attached bonus compensation to achieving what team members in my business said they would do to get where they said they wanted to be. If someone wanted to move to a more senior role in the organization, for example, we would look at competencies they would need to develop and break those skills into small pieces that could be accomplished in the next quarter. If someone wanted to build their presentation skills, we could have them begin to work on the outline of a presentation or view a YouTube video that could be instructive.

I was careful to have the PDP action steps solely within the person's control. For example, if someone wanted to gain a certain competency around client acquisition, we would set the action step to be making a certain number of sales calls as opposed to setting an action step of gaining a certain number of new clients. They couldn't control who bought, but they could control their own actions.

We always made sure the actions set were capable of being accomplished. Did the person have the knowledge and skills to complete the task? If not, we backed up and set a preliminary action step to gain the needed knowledge or skills.

As important as their competency was, they needed to be motivated to work on the action steps. If I had done my job right — as in, listened to what they wanted and aligned and recentered the action steps with their values — motivation was usually not a problem.

ANY PROCESS
WORTH ITS SALT
EVENTUALLY
IS REDUCED
INTO ACTION.

Review Progress

Ninety days from the current meeting, we could check progress and make any adjustments to the plan. Often, I would help set up an employee's goal that required collaboration with someone else. This was intentional because having an accountability partner is important. If you are implementing your plan, reviewing and adjusting progress is critical to staying on track.

GOAL ACTIONS

Now that you've seen the process, it's time to think about putting it into action for yourself.

1. **Define your vision and values.** Take some time to clearly define and identify a vision of your future that *truly matters* to you. Start by writing down your values. Then, begin to imagine the next plateau.

2. **Break down your journey to your next plateau into actionable steps.** Once you have your short-term goals, break them down into small, manageable tasks or milestones. This will make them less overwhelming and allow you to track your progress more effectively.

1. **Put these goals through your own acid test.** Can you afford to achieve these goals in terms of time and energy? Are you both *willing* and *able* to achieve these goals?

2. **Create and implement a plan.** Develop a well-structured plan that outlines the specific actions (how, where, when) that you need to take to achieve your short-term goals. Set realistic deadlines and create a timeline for each step along the way.

3. **Seek support and accountability.** Share your goals with someone you trust, such as a close friend, family member, or mentor. Allow this support relationship to help you make corrections to your plan as needed.

Making substantive changes in your goals requires commitment, patience, and perseverance. Celebrate small victories along the way, and be open to adjusting your approach as needed. Stay focused on your desired outcomes and believe in your ability to bring about meaningful change in your life.

PLATEAU-JUMPING QUESTIONS

What goal would you pursue if you were guaranteed to fail, but the process and journey itself brought you immense joy and fulfillment?

If you could wake up tomorrow having gained any skill or ability, what would it be? How would that impact your goals?

If you had all the financial resources and time available, how would you spend your days? How can you incorporate elements of that vision into your current goals?

Imagine yourself five years from now. What goals and actions would your future self tell you to prioritize and pursue?

What goals have you hesitated to pursue due to fear of judgment or criticism from others?

What small, incremental, short-term goals could guide you in the direction of your next plateau? Do they pass the acid test?

Remember, these questions are meant to provoke deep reflection and provide guidance. I know there are a lot of questions here. Take it slow. Take your time to contemplate them and allow your answers to guide you toward making meaningful changes in your goals.

CHAPTER 8

Plateau Relationships

LISTENING JUMPS TALKING

"Things are never quite as scary when you've got a best friend."
— BILL WATTERSON, CREATOR OF *CALVIN AND HOBBES*

"The key is to keep company only with people who uplift you, whose presence calls forth your best." — EPICTETUS, PHILOSOPHER

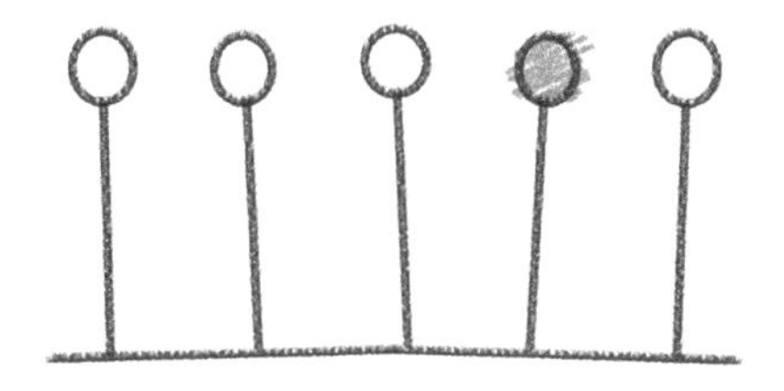

BICYCLES AND BOXING

FOR ALMOST ANY young boy, a bicycle represents freedom. When you are on your bike, you have independence. You are in control.

During the 1940s and 50s, a segregated Louisville, Kentucky, was a difficult place to feel free and independent if you were a black child. In 1954, a twelve-year-old black boy named Cassius Clay had some of that freedom taken away when his new red Schwinn bicycle was stolen outside the Louisville Home Show.

Distraught, enraged, and unsure of what to do, he reported the theft to a nearby police officer named Joe Martin. Furious, Clay was shouting, "I'm gonna whup those boys that took my bike!" He wanted a fight, and he wanted it now.

But what happened next would change Clay's life forever.

There was something Clay, along with many others, didn't know about Officer Martin. Martin had a bigger purpose — he was not just a police officer. He was also a professional boxer with a record of 15-3-1.

Speaking from experience and his deeper purpose, Martin suggested, "Maybe you should learn how to fight before you go looking for one." When he invited Clay to join his after-school boxing club, Clay accepted.

As a professional boxer himself, Martin knew the value of hard work and determination in the ring. He had seen something in Clay that he recognized from his own early years in the sport — a fierce determination to succeed despite the odds. It was this recognition that led him to take the young boy under his wing and teach him everything he knew about boxing.

Clay trained at the Columbia Gym in Louisville, where he was surrounded by other boxers who became like family to him. Not yet the athlete he would become, Clay initially struggled with the sport, never intending to become a professional boxer. Training was simply a way to learn to defend himself. He was a skinny kid who didn't have the natural athleticism that many of the other boxers had. But he had heart, and he worked harder than anyone else to improve his skills. He would stay at the gym for hours after training, simply watching the older boxers spar and absorbing as much knowledge as he could.

As he began to win more matches and gain recognition, his love for the sport grew. His passion followed his competency. In 1960, Clay won a gold medal at the Olympics in Rome, and his boxing career took off. He won his first professional fight that same year. By 1964, he had become the world heavyweight champion, defeating Sonny Liston in one of the most famous fights in boxing history. His victory over Liston marked the beginning of a period of his dominance in the sport. From there, he went on to become one of the most successful boxers of all time, with a record of 56-5 and countless titles and awards. He eventually changed his name to Muhammad Ali. Ali would become an iconic figure in sports history and American culture.

But it all started with a stolen red Schwinn bicycle and a police officer with a purpose who saw something special in a young boy and was willing to form a relationship. The story of Cassius Clay and Joe Martin is a testament to the power of relationships.

If we want to change our plateau, one of the levers we may have to change is our relationships. But how? We can start by looking outward in the same way Joe Martin did when he changed a twelve-year-old boy's life trajectory. It starts with seeking to find what the other person wants and to serve them.

Knowing how to do that starts with better questions and, more importantly, better listening. Listen for what the other person needs. Help them get what they want.

It starts with empathy.

LISTEN WITH EMPATHY: ASK BETTER QUESTIONS

Relationships are the most important things in life. Master them, and you'll master the journey. This journey includes our relationships with family members, friends, co-workers, God, and ourselves. It requires understanding and self-awareness. It requires primarily listening with an empathetic ear to others and to the voice inside us.

One way to change your relationships is to change how you listen.

Listening for the Enemy

In early 2021, we had the pleasure of hosting Eric Maddox on the *Decidedly* podcast.[51] You might not be familiar with his name, but his story is etched in history.

Maddox served as the lead interrogator for the US Army after the invasion of Iraq in 2003. The clock was ticking, however, and Maddox was faced with a daunting task — finding high-value target number one, Saddam Hussein — before Maddox would get his orders to leave Iraq.

The traditional methods employed by the US Army at the time were falling short. Prisoners were stonewalling Maddox. He was getting nowhere. Maddox was running out of time, and it seemed like he would return home empty-handed. But he had an unexpected idea — he decided to change his approach to interrogation. The key? Listening.

Maddox set aside his own agenda, embraced empathy, and started asking better questions. It was a game-changer.

One lead led to another, and then another, like an intricate puzzle coming together. Eventually, Maddox and his

RELATIONSHIPS
ARE THE
MOST IMPORTANT
THINGS IN LIFE.
MASTER THEM, AND
YOU'LL MASTER
THE JOURNEY.

team discovered Hussein hiding in a small hole at a farmhouse near the town of Ad-Dawr. The army had searched the location and found nothing. As they were preparing to leave, the prisoner Maddox had interrogated and sent with them motioned to a small rope that led to the trap door covering the hole where Hussein was hiding. The prisoner, a member of Hussein's inner circle, had the information Maddox needed. All it took was listening. It was a remarkable conclusion to a journey that began with the simple act of truly listening, setting his own agenda aside, and understanding the perspectives of others.

If you want to hear the full story (and you should), I recommend checking out episodes eight and nine of the *Decidedly* podcast. Maddox's account is a testament to the power of empathy and the importance of stepping outside our own preconceptions to find the truth.

EMPATHIC LISTENING TIPS

You can significantly enhance your empathetic listening skills and establish a foundation of trust and understanding in your relationships by just setting aside your own agenda and asking better questions. Your questions are not meant to turn a conversation into an interview but to listen for what that person is truly trying to share with you.

Sometimes, what a person is trying to share is not immediately accessible, even to them. They just start talking, and then small clues emerge, revealing imprecise language that needs to be explored. Listen for absolutes that connect

SOMETIMES, WHAT A PERSON IS TRYING TO SHARE IS NOT IMMEDIATELY ACCESSIBLE, EVEN TO THEM.

to feelings, adjectives that need exploration, or even words or concepts that keep showing up.

I've found two questions that have proved useful in connecting.

"Tell Me More About That"

All right, I know it's not a question. But it is so simple and yet effective.

Years ago, a client of mine was considering a Plateau Jump. She wanted to open a clothing store. She had no background in fashion and no experience in the retail business. She had just left a successful sales job in advertising and had saved some money.

She described the idea, stating, "I want to open a small boutique for women." I listened and kept asking questions.

"Oh, tell me more about that."

As I probed, she kept coming to dead ends. The idea wasn't passing the affordability test. She wasn't willing and able to put in the time, energy, and resources needed to start the business. Having no prior experience in the field, she lacked the capabilities as well.

It was the wrong plateau. We both saw that.

"What Would You Like to See Happen?"

Often, we listen and offer advice when advice isn't what is needed.

I am in a business group where offering advice is prohibited. Sounds counterintuitive, but it works. We meet for half a day each month. Someone will present an issue they are dealing with or a dilemma they are facing. Our role is not to offer advice but to ask questions.

We fire off questions like: "What would a new buyer of your business do?" "What are your instincts telling you?" "In five years, what will you wish you would have done?" "It seems like you know what to do; why aren't you doing it?" The questions just keep coming.

What we have found is that:

- If we offer advice rather than asking questions, it robs the person of developing their own responsibility for the answer.
- Likewise, if we offer a solution that turns out not to work, it inappropriately absolves that person of personal responsibility for their actions.
- If we offer advice that isn't taken, it may create resentment and a reluctance to engage in the future.

So, we just ask, and then we listen. We ask, "What would you like to see happen?" Many times, they don't know. "Hmm, tell me more about that."

If you are doing this for someone else, you can bounce between these two questions and versions of these questions and not only learn more about what they are thinking and feeling but also what they want. If you keep listening and asking questions, the resolution will reveal itself.

Remember: Change takes time and effort, so be patient with yourself and others. Consistency and a commitment to personal growth are key.

Changing relationships isn't always a positive thing, either. I had a client years ago who was comfortable changing relationships — perhaps too comfortable. He changed jobs and spouses so often that it was creating a severe threat to his own financial stability. He kept starting over and halving his net worth in the process. He wasn't improving his life through these changes. What he wanted to see happen was not happening — but he didn't realize why.

If you want change, then changing the nature of relationships or the relationships themselves is a powerfully necessary tool. However, remember that sometimes, changing relationships should start with your relationship with yourself. You may need to understand more about yourself before you try understanding or helping others.

When that is the case, go back to the mindsets we discussed earlier in this book. Start with gratitude for the fact that you can reset and jump forward from there.

JUST ASK

A few years ago, at a conference in Washington, DC, I heard an amazing speaker named Jia Jiang. (If you want to see his message, you can find it on YouTube in a video titled "What I Learned from 100 Days of Rejection." As of the writing of this book, it has been viewed over ten million times.)

Jai decided to see what random people would do for him if he just asked. He created a list of outrageous requests.

"Can I borrow $100?" was one of his first requests from a stranger. Rejected! But he kept on making crazy requests. He expected rejection, and he got plenty. That wasn't the surprising part.

The surprising part was the extraordinary things that happened simply because he asked. When he asked, many people said yes. He drove a police car. He taught a college class. He played soccer in a stranger's yard with him. He was a greeter at Starbucks. The list goes on.

He changed his relationships with the people he encountered, transforming them from strangers to allies. He created meaningful relationships where none existed. What a terrific way to Plateau Jump.

A SIMPLE REQUEST

Since we are discussing relationships in this chapter, I thought I would change my relationship with myself and embrace the fear of rejection. If you've made it this far in the book, either you're my mother, or you're someone who is getting something out of what you are reading. Either way, I hope you are enjoying the experience of reading *Plateau Jumping*. My guess is there are other people who would get something from this book as well.

What makes the book easier to find on Amazon and other booksellers online is reviews. So, can I ask you a favor? Can you leave an online review? It takes only a few seconds and costs nothing, and it would mean so much to me. Maybe because of the reviews, someone will find this book. Maybe they'll read this book. And that someone, who neither of us know, will make their own Plateau Jump. Imagine that!

RELATIONSHIP ACTIONS

Here are some ways you can immediately start changing and adding to your relationships.

1. **Enhance your own self-awareness.** Start by cultivating self-awareness through introspection and reflection. Take time to understand your own values, needs, and boundaries within relationships.

2. **Improve your communication skills.** Communication is key to healthy relationships. Work on developing effective communication skills, such as empathetic listening. Put yourself in the other person's shoes and set your own agenda aside. Ask better questions.

3. **Foster growth and support.** Encourage personal growth and support in your relationships. Celebrate the successes and achievements of others and offer your support and encouragement during challenging times. Create an environment that promotes growth, understanding, and collaboration.

By implementing these action steps, you can proactively improve the quality of your relationships and create a positive and nurturing environment for yourself and those around you.

PLATEAU-JUMPING QUESTIONS

How do you actively listen and empathize with others in your relationships? What can you do to enhance your communication skills to deepen your connections?

What do you need more of in your relationships to make your next Plateau Jump?

What do you need less of in your relationships to make your next Plateau Jump?

How might your own fears and insecurities influence the way you engage in your relationships, and how can you address them?

What limiting beliefs or negative self-perceptions do you hold that might be influencing the dynamics of your relationships? How can you challenge and overcome them?

CHAPTER 9

Plateau Beliefs

OPEN JUMPS CLOSED

"Your beliefs become your thoughts, your thoughts become your words, your words become your actions, your actions become your habits, your habits become your values, your values become your destiny." — MAHATMA GANDHI

"Progress is impossible without change, and those that cannot change their minds cannot change anything." — GEORGE BERNARD SHAW

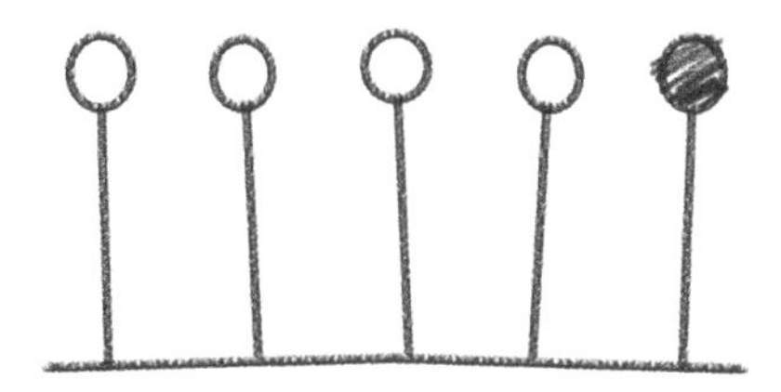

AS I BEGAN drafting this book on personal change, I found myself confronted with a challenge that left me feeling overwhelmed. Over lunch one day, I sat with my father, excitedly sharing the concepts of Plateau Jumping that I had been

exploring. I explained how plateaus were natural spaces for learning and reflection and how we could use specific levers to purposefully propel ourselves from one plateau to the next.

As I discussed my research, I proudly mentioned the *four* levers I had identified: systems, habits, goals, and relationships. It was then that my father, playing his PhD in psychology card, gently pointed out, "You missed one: beliefs."

His words struck me with a sense of realization. He was right. If we are to make a Plateau Jump, of course, one of the levers you might need to pull would be changing your own beliefs.

I later shared this conversation with my friend David, seeking solace in what I hoped would be a shared agreement about the difficulty of changing beliefs. To me, it seemed like an insurmountable task to guide someone through such a profound transformation.

"How do we even recognize the need to change our beliefs if we lack the self-awareness to perceive it?" I wondered aloud.

David, who happens to be the pastor of a large church in Fort Worth, responded with an air of confidence. He dealt with discussions on changing beliefs daily; it was his business, after all.

"Oh, changing beliefs is easy," he reassured me, "but it needs to be incremental." He explained how his experience had taught him to approach the process gradually and with care.

My concerns persisted. "But how can I possibly include a chapter on changing beliefs without merely scratching the surface of such a profound topic? Changing one's beliefs could fill an entire book. Entire religions are founded on this very premise!"

The weight of this dilemma hung heavy in the air as I contemplated the magnitude of what it meant to change one's beliefs. How would someone know which beliefs to change? It was clear that addressing this subject required a delicate balance between depth and brevity, encompassing the intricacies of belief systems without trivializing their significance. Changing your own beliefs is about more than just rearranging your own biases — it's about defeating them.

FIND THE UNRECOGNIZED PROBLEM

Several years back, I found myself immersed in advisory work for a family with a unique possession: a roadside attraction known as a show cave. This subterranean wonderland beckoned explorers to venture beneath the surface, revealing the captivating beauty that remained concealed from the world above. It was like a secret waiting to be unlocked.

Over time, the family had added additional features to the overall attraction. Ziplines, miniature golf, and even a small museum were all woven into the landscape, aiming to elevate the attraction's appeal. Yet, despite their efforts, growth proved steady but slow. They enhanced the visitors' experiences, upgrading the gift shop and adding a sprawling playground for kids to explore. Still, progress remained gradual.

However, in one pivotal year, a game-changer emerged from a seemingly mundane act: expanding the parking lot into an adjacent expanse of vacant land near the entrance. In a remarkable twist, this shift ignited an unprecedented surge in business. The realization was astonishing. People craved something that had gone unrecognized — accessibility. The underlying marvel was captivating, but limited parking hindered the discovery. As the parking lot brimmed with vehicles, it became evident that accessibility was key. When the hidden gem was made reachable, it drew visitors like moths to a flame.

Your positive beliefs mirror this phenomenon. While on the one hand, they are akin to the treasures nestled in the cave below the surface, waiting to be shared with the world, on the other hand, they can remain hidden. These beliefs, often residing beneath the visible exterior, possess the potential to unite you with those who may share your journey. Like a beacon, they will beckon those you encounter, inviting them to glimpse what lies beneath the surface. Yet, if you don't make them accessible to others, you will not find those connections. And if your beliefs and values lie in internal places that even *you* don't try to get to, they are doubly hidden.

In essence, like the cave's concealed wonders, your positive values and beliefs possess the magic to draw people toward you, unveiling the captivating realm that resides below the surface. Your task is to uncover and clarify them, making them accessible to yourself and others.

TRANSFORM YOUR BELIEFS

A surprising study by Harvard psychologist Ellen Langer challenged the conventional understanding of the mind-body relationship and the power of beliefs and perception.[52] Langer's study focused on hotel maids, who spend their days engaged in physically demanding tasks, yet, surprisingly, most of them didn't perceive themselves as physically active. Even more puzzling, their bodies did not seem to benefit from their daily exertions despite exceeding the recommended daily exercise levels.

Driven by curiosity, Langer decided to change these maids' beliefs and perceptions. She educated one group about the calories burned during their daily activities, enlightening them about their already active lifestyle. Most believed that their work activity did not count as exercise. Langer told them that it did. The other group received no such information and continued as before.

A month later, the results astounded everyone. The group who believed their work activity counted as exercise displayed a significant decrease in systolic blood pressure, weight, and waist-to-hip ratio. Their blood pressure had dropped by an impressive 10 percent. Surprisingly, there was no evidence that the maids altered their routines or behaviors, leading Langer to attribute the change to their transformed mindset.

This intriguing phenomenon is akin to the placebo effect, where belief in receiving treatment can lead to actual improvements in health, even when the treatment itself is a mere sugar pill. The study challenges the notion of "objective reality" in the physical body and suggests that if you genuinely believe you are exercising, your body might respond accordingly.

You probably won't be so lucky as to drop a few pounds in the next month because some Harvard researchers tell you what you're already doing counts as exercise. Keep hope alive, but that probably won't happen. Instead, explore the following practices, which can help you in many ways.

Self-Awareness

As we touched on in the goals and relationships sections, we must become conscious of our existing beliefs and their influence on our thoughts, emotions, and behaviors. You can't change if you don't know what needs to be changed. You can't know what needs to be changed if you don't recognize what you are feeling or what you really want. Self-aware people can recognize what they are feeling, make sense of those feelings, and regulate their emotions and actions.

Questioning the origins of your attitudes and emotions and evaluating the evidence supporting them allows you to challenge biases and limitations. This boils down to thinking about what you think about. Being mindful of what you are mindful of. Journaling helps. Exploring the question of what you are thinking and feeling throughout the day is useful. It helps you become aware.

I have a friend who sets an alarm on his phone to go off during the day. When it does, he stops and explores what he is thinking and feeling at that moment. For leaders and parents, this is particularly important. You can't help someone else deal with something until you've dealt with yourself. Do this, and you'll begin asking better questions, not just of others but of yourself. But you must also be willing to answer those questions.

Openness

Next, intentional exposure plays a vital role. By actively seeking out diverse viewpoints, experiences, and sources of information, you broaden your perspectives and challenge the rigidity of your existing beliefs. Engaging in open-minded discussions and embracing alternative perspectives fuels your intellectual curiosity and fosters personal development.

It starts with being open to new ideas about things you already know to be true. For example, if I asked you if one and one equals two, you would likely respond in the affirmative. But if I add one cloud to another, I have only one cloud. If I add one dirt pile to another, I have only one dirt pile. One plus one may not always equal two. Openness, then, is a mindset of knowing for sure that you don't know for sure.

Each Sunday, I have a group text with my children. Each week, I send a question for them to think over and respond to. We have kept this string of questions and answers going for years. They are sometimes simple questions, like, "What book are you reading next?" or "What are you proud of?" Sometimes, they are deeper: "What did you need more of growing up?"

One of the questions I found most difficult to answer for myself was this: "When we look at the political landscape, we see people on the other side who have clearly been misled by their political party or news media into believing things that are not true. What do I believe that may not be true?" If you really want to challenge your own beliefs, ask yourself that question.

Remember the Harvard University (or was it Yale?) goals study we discussed in Chapter 7? You remember; it claimed that writing down your goals produced 10 times your income twenty years after graduation.

Turns out the study is an urban myth. People have referred to it in their articles because they found it in other articles, but no one went to find the actual study. It's something we want to believe, but the twenty-year study does not exist.

"WHAT DO I BELIEVE THAT MAY NOT BE TRUE?" IF YOU REALLY WANT TO CHALLENGE YOUR OWN BELIEFS, ASK YOURSELF THAT QUESTION.

This doesn't make the advice of writing down your goals invalid. The good news is that a study on the issue showing the benefits of written goals was eventually performed. We will look at those results in a later chapter.

Reframing

Reinterpretation is another powerful tool that advances openness. By reframing and reinterpreting situations, we create new meanings and perspectives. This process enables us to challenge limiting beliefs and find alternative explanations. By embracing setbacks as opportunities for growth and adopting a mindset of possibilities, we can navigate the transformative landscape of belief.

Often, we judge our own actions by our intentions but judge others by their actions alone. What if you were to consider the possibility that someone may have had benevolent intentions? What if we attributed incompetence instead of malevolence to their actions?

Curiosity

We've already talked about curiosity as a motivation, but it's also useful in changing our beliefs. Cultivating curiosity ignites a passion for exploration and inquiry. By approaching our beliefs with a sense of wonder and openness, we can question assumptions, seek new knowledge, and challenge our own perspectives. Embracing unconventional questions and actively seeking diverse sources of information fuel our intellectual curiosity and propel us toward continuous learning and growth.

"It's not what we don't know that gets us in trouble, it's what we know for sure that just ain't so." —Mark Twain

You may have noticed that I have included many questions for you to ask yourself throughout this book. We become better able to exist on the next plateau not by simply gaining competencies or envisioning climbing the Wall of Change but by asking better questions. If you have been skipping over those questions I have included (yes, I'm talking to you), go back and answer them. Until you do, you will not gain the introspective skills needed to examine your own beliefs.

Mark Twain is famously quoted as saying, "It's not what we don't know that gets us in trouble, it's what we know for sure that just ain't so." Often, the things we are certain about and take for granted are the things that can cause us the most trouble. It's not the things we are ignorant about that are the problem, but rather the things we are confident we know but which are incorrect. Those might even be self-limiting beliefs about your ability to jump to the next plateau.

By integrating these practices into our journey of belief transformation, we empower ourselves to positively impact our beliefs and embark on a path of personal development. This approach, encompassing self-awareness, openness, reframing, and curiosity, unlocks the potential for transformative growth and enhances our understanding of the world and ourselves.

BELIEF ACTIONS

Now, it is time for you to start working on changing your own beliefs. Here are some actions to take to begin this process:

1. **Engage in self-reflection.** Dedicate regular time for introspection and self-reflection. Create a journal or a reflective practice through which you can explore your beliefs, identify patterns, and examine their origins. Ask yourself thought-provoking questions, and be honest in your reflections.

2. **Explore contradictory perspectives.** Purposely seek out evidence or experiences that challenge your existing beliefs. Be willing to question the validity of your current beliefs and explore alternative interpretations. Look for information that supports different viewpoints and consider their potential value. You know where you can go to get the news commentary that confirms your beliefs. Now, take a moment (if you can stand it) to seek new information from the opposing source.

3. **Embrace a growth mindset.** Adopt a mindset that emphasizes the belief that your abilities and intelligence can be developed over time. Embrace the idea that your beliefs are not fixed and can evolve as you learn and grow.

Those who will not change their beliefs voluntarily will eventually be compelled to do so by the sheer weight of the consequences those beliefs bring about. They will find themselves at the Canyon Wall. From your self-aware vantage point, however, you can see those consequences coming if you look.

THOSE WHO WILL
NOT CHANGE THEIR
BELIEFS VOLUNTARILY
WILL EVENTUALLY
BE COMPELLED TO
DO SO BY THE SHEER
WEIGHT OF THE
CONSEQUENCES
THOSE BELIEFS
BRING ABOUT.

What can I do to challenge my own beliefs?

What beliefs am I currently holding onto that no longer serve my growth and well-being? How are these beliefs limiting me from embracing new opportunities?

How can I actively seek out information, experiences, and conversations that challenge my existing beliefs?

What should I be curious about at the next plateau and ask more questions?

How does fear play a role in maintaining my current beliefs that hold me back?

CHAPTER 10

Combining the Levers

STRENGTH JUMPS WEAKNESS

"The secret of change is to focus all of your energy not on fighting the old, but on building the new." — SOCRATES

"It is not the strongest or the most intelligent who will survive but those who can best manage change." — CHARLES DARWIN

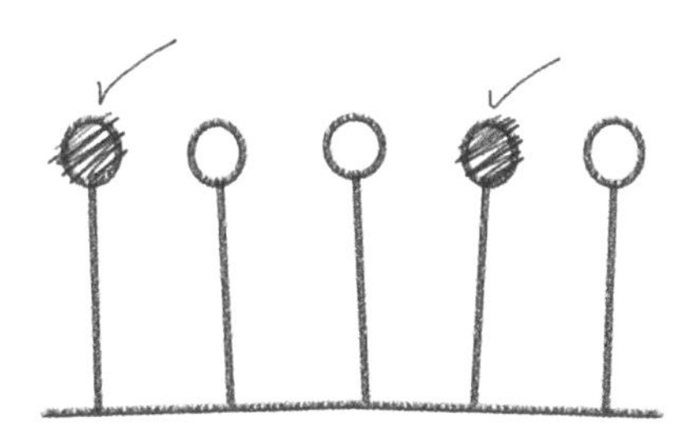

YOU'VE ENVISIONED A new plateau for yourself. But you can't change what is happening around you without changing some of the fundamental aspects of you. Those are the Levers of Change. But which lever to pull?

Selecting a lever to pull can seem daunting. Most people I speak with who are looking at a big change are at a point nearing the Canyon Wall and are feeling the pressure of external forces. Those forces work their destructive magic on the weakest parts. They seek out your vulnerabilities.

It's natural, then, that we would want to bolster those weaknesses. "Hey, my systems are a mess! I should work on improving my systems!" "I have some bad habits to fix; let's change those first."

I'm going to suggest that you take the opposite approach. If your systems are terrible, it's probably because you're terrible at systems. If you don't have a lot of social support or long-term friends or employees, relationships may not be your strength. Ok, you already knew these things, but someone had to say it out loud. There. I said it.

FOCUS ON YOUR STRENGTHS

I'm not saying not to work on what is broken. If you have an inadequacy preventing you from reaching the next plateau, you clearly must address it. But if you have areas where you just don't excel, working on those least strong areas will have marginal benefits.

How much time did Tom Brady spend on tackling? Not much. Sure, it's part of the game. There were times when he had to do it, but getting better at it wasn't what made him great. Should he have worked on his long passes? He doesn't crack the top 150 all-time in yards per pass completed. Yet he has more passing yards than anyone in the history of the game. His strength was his ability to read the defenses and exploit mismatches.

You have strengths, and they operate in the opposite of the areas you want to improve. Maybe you have a hard time following systems, but that's because you see ways to cut through the bureaucracy. Maybe you can't stand getting into the details, but that's because you more easily see the big picture. Maybe you don't like uncertainty, but that dislike causes you to make fewer mistakes.

Leverage those strengths. In fact, it's those strengths that will get you to the next plateau. Working on your weaknesses will only make you slightly less terrible in those areas. Amplify your strengths, and you can make a difference.

With all due respect to Marshall Goldsmith's book *What Got You Here Won't Get You There*[53], the instinctual strengths that got you here will indeed get you there.

Goldsmith's book is centered on the idea that the very habits and behaviors that have contributed to an individual's past successes might be the same ones holding them back from achieving even greater success in the future. Your instinctual strengths, such as predispositions and inherent abilities, are what got you here. Your instinctual strengths must get you there. The reason is they don't change.

How you interact with facts and figures, systems, uncertainty, and the physical world around you are part of your strengths. Some things will feel natural to you. They should; they're the ones that work for you. Don't change those things.

Amplify your opportunities to utilize those strengths in your jump. If you are a "systems person," then make sure Systems is a lever you are pulling to jump. If you are a "people person," then the Relationships Lever is one you'll want to pull to make the jump.

To fully utilize your strengths to move to the next plateau, you need to know what those strengths are. Kathy Kolbe, founder of Kolbe Corp., has done some revolutionary work on this topic and has created several self-assessment tools.[54] We had a wide-ranging discussion on the topic of strengths on *Decidedly* when Amy Bruske, president of Kolbe Corp., was our guest.[55] You can learn more about your instinctual strengths at www.kolbe.com.

COMBINE TWO LEVERS FOR GREATER POWER

When evaluating the levers in the pursuit of personal change and growth, it is often tempting to rely on a single approach or lever. However, using two levers simultaneously can produce a remarkable synergistic effect, leading to enhanced outcomes and a more comprehensive transformation.

You instinctively know where your strengths exist. Now, double down on those. Let's pair a Strength Lever with a Support Lever to act as an accountability point and backstop.

Imagine you are making a Plateau Jump, and you have outstanding habits. You're known for them. You eat right, work out, and do your daily meditation. You've got this. Why not focus on making a new habit that will take you to the next plateau? On top of that, imagine if you paired that with a change in relationship so that you had an accountability partner or a goal to develop a new positive habit each quarter.

Here's another example. Imagine you are making a Plateau Jump, and you are great at setting and achieving goals. You write them down. You post them on a vision board. You could amplify your impact by adding a system to track progress or working on creating a belief that your goals could be bigger. Pairing or combining multiple areas of change can enable them to work together synergistically, adding great value.

When preparing your Plateau Jump, you'll want to pull the Lever of Change that aligns with your strength and then select a secondary lever as support. They essentially act in tandem, with a primary lever based on your strengths and a secondary lever based on compatibility with your strengths.

The following are a few levers that pair well together. You'll notice your own as you begin to practice the approach. Don't get too tied into one approach. You've likely got more than one strong lever to pull, so allow the jump itself to inform which of your strengths to utilize.

Goals Plus Relationships

Now, let's go back to our "Harvard" urban myth study on having vague goals versus having specific written goals. It turns out, to no one's surprise, that writing down the specific goals does help. What's interesting is that if you add a relationship component, such as an accountability partner who sees your goals and your progress, goal achievement goes up by 77 percent.[56]

Companies like Noom have figured this out. Noom is a weight loss app that uses a combination of Plateau-Jumping approaches and Levers of Change. Users start by entering a *goal* into the app. They have a three-color *system* for identifying foods. Users create *habits* of weighing themselves and logging caloric intake each day. There are articles users read to challenge their *beliefs*.

Noom also wisely uses *relationships* by incorporating small accountability groups as well as personal coaches. Studies have shown that those who participated in a Plateau Jump of weight loss reported that coaching helped them become accustomed to eating healthier (68 percent coached vs. 54 percent not coached) and helped them to increase their physical activity (71 percent vs. 45 percent).[57] Even just using a couple of these approaches paired together will yield better results than going it alone or never declaring the Plateau Jump goal in the first place.

Goals Plus Beliefs

The first step to changing your goals is believing you are someone who reaches your goals. Aligning your goals with empowering beliefs can be a potent combination. When your beliefs are congruent with your goals and aspirations, they provide the motivation, confidence, and self-efficacy to pursue and achieve your goals. Positive beliefs can reinforce your commitment and resilience along the journey.

Goals Plus Systems

Setting clear short-term goals and implementing supportive systems can work together synergistically. Goals provide direction and a sense of purpose, while systems provide the practical framework to achieve those goals. By pairing these areas, you ensure that your goals are supported by actionable steps and strategies.

Systems Plus Habits

Developing effective systems while nurturing empowering habits can create a solid foundation for personal growth.

Systems provide the structure and processes for taking consistent action, while habits ensure consistent behaviors. By aligning these two aspects, you can create a powerful framework for sustained behavior change and increased productivity.

Creating supportive systems, such as setting up a conducive environment or establishing specific routines, can help intentional habit formation, reinforcing your desired changes and making them more automatic over time. Developing effective systems and implementing supportive habits go hand in hand. Systems provide structure and organization, while habits ensure consistent action.

Habits Plus Relationships

Cultivating positive habits within the embrace of supportive relationships fosters a nurturing environment that offers accountability, encouragement, and social support. These pillars become instrumental in the adoption and maintenance of new habits. Look at the success of organizations such as Alcoholics Anonymous, for example.

WHY COMBINING LEVERS WORKS

Strategically combining two levers gives you advantages you wouldn't have otherwise.

Enhanced Synergy

Combining two Levers of Change creates a synergistic effect, where the benefits of each approach reinforce and amplify one another. This synergy maximizes the impact and effectiveness of the overall change process. You may have heard the often-told example of the Belgian horses. One Belgian horse can pull 8,000 pounds, but if yoked together with another, both horses can now pull 24,000. Seems like it should only be 16,000 pounds, right?

Why is it over twice the amount each could pull independently? Interestingly, if you yoke two horses and train them together, the weight increases to nearly 32,000 pounds. Maybe it's the desire to demonstrate dominance, the excitement of teamwork, or the ability to create greater inertia, but whatever the reason, the synergistic effect is noticeably present.

Holistic Approach

When contemplating change, we tend to focus on a single approach, hoping it will deliver the desired results. By recognizing complementary tools, we open ourselves up to a more holistic transformation.

Let's go back to our example of weight loss. Rather than solely relying on either exercise or diet, combining the two creates a more comprehensive strategy. Exercise boosts metabolism, builds strength, and improves overall health, while a well-balanced diet nourishes our bodies and supports sustainable weight loss. When we unite these tools, their combined effects surpass what each could achieve individually. This makes sense, right?

This works for your Levers of Change as well. Think about combining cognitive, behavioral, and social strategies. Cognitive strategies like shifting your thought patterns are represented in your goals and beliefs. Behavioral strategies show up in your systems and habits. Social strategies appear through changing the nature of and types of relationships.

Combining approaches provides a more comprehensive and well-rounded perspective on your Plateau Jump. By targeting multiple aspects simultaneously, you address various dimensions of the desired change, leading to a more holistic transformation.[58]

Amplified Commitment

When we commit to change, it's easy to lose focus or become overwhelmed by distractions. The internal accountability structure plays a crucial role by serving as a commitment amplifier. By selecting two complementary tools, we establish a dynamic interplay that reinforces our commitment and propels us forward.

When you think of a Plateau Jump you are seeking, you will naturally want to begin to look at the lever to pull to effect that change. But begin to think of it as selecting two levers to pull in tandem. One primary and one supporting. Your primary Lever of Change should be selected based on your personal strengths. The secondary lever should relate to the circumstances of the change.

In the pursuit of your next plateau, there lies an inherent value in the convergence of multiple areas of change, harmonizing them in a synergistic symphony. By seamlessly integrating different Levers of Change, such as systems, habits, goals, relationships, and beliefs, you can transcend the boundaries of isolated efforts and embrace a holistic approach to your Plateau Jump.

STRENGTHS ACTION

Consider taking an assessment such as the Kolbe A™ Index[59], which highlights your instinctive strengths. These are the natural strengths that got you where you are. These are the strengths that are not likely to change. Align your jump to utilize those instincts.

Why does this matter? Try something: Grab a pen and write your name. Now, switch the pen to the opposite hand and try it again. What did you notice? Did it seem awkward, take longer, yield worse results? That's the result you will get in your Plateau Jump if you are not aligned with your instinctual strengths. Knowing what they are is the first step.

PLATEAU-JUMPING QUESTIONS

Which Lever of Change is my strength?

Which areas - cognitive, behavioral, or social - do I believe will have the greatest impact on my personal growth and transformation?

How can I integrate these Levers of Change to work together synergistically?

What specific goals can I set within each of these areas to guide my progress?

What systems or habits can I establish to support and reinforce the changes I want to make?

How can I leverage my relationships and beliefs to enhance and amplify the effects of these two areas of change?

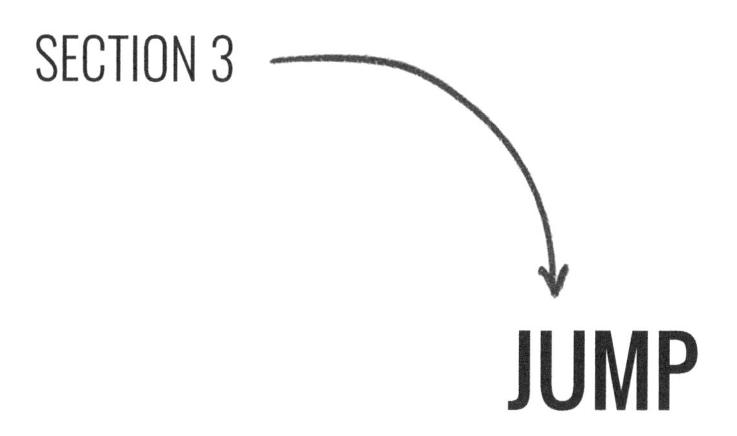

Navigating the landscape is challenging, but you can take shortcuts if you know what you're looking for and how to make the most of the whole process. Life becomes more rewarding if you learn when and how to jump more quickly from one plateau to the next, avoiding many of the obstacles and achieving more of the desired growth.

CHAPTER 11

Finding Your Next Plateau

CLARITY JUMPS UNCERTAINTY

"Your values are like your fingerprints. Nobody's are the same, but you leave 'em all over everything you do." — ELVIS PRESLEY

"Dreams can become a reality when we possess a vision, a plan, and the courage to chase it relentlessly." — WALT DISNEY

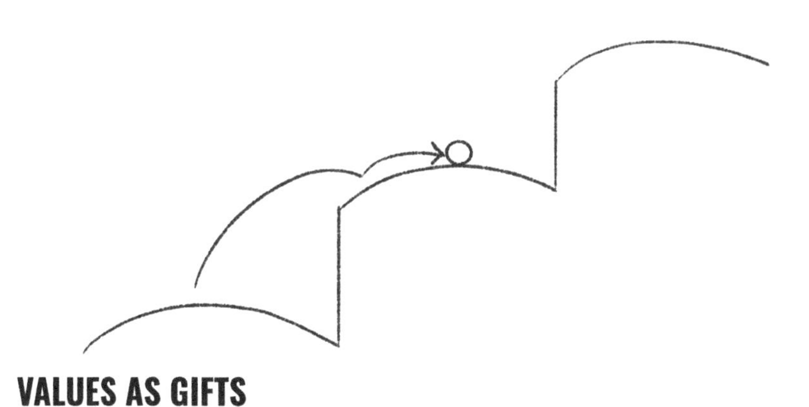

VALUES AS GIFTS

WHEN NATALIA MATVEEVA, entrepreneur and founder of Peak Genesis Mentoring, joined Sanger and me on the *Decidedly* podcast[60], she said, "I shouldn't be here."

For a moment, I thought she meant she shouldn't be on the podcast. What she meant was that she shouldn't be alive.

When the Chernobyl Nuclear Power Plant disaster occurred on April 26, 1986, Natalia was living within the exclusion zone, the area immediately around the site of the world's worst nuclear disaster. This area is still uninhabitable today. It was forcibly evacuated in the days following the disaster.

The silhouette of the plant on the horizon was a familiar fixture in town. Living in proximity to a nuclear power plant seemed normal until Russian officials showed up and told Natalia's parents that the state was providing a getaway to a nearby lake resort for the town residents. No need to pack anything. The buses loaded up, and she and her family were driven away. They were never allowed to return. Their belongings were highly contaminated with radioactivity, which explains why they were forbidden to pack anything to take with them.

Unfortunately, Natalia was also contaminated with the same radiation. At the age of seven, Natalia was told by her doctors that she would live perhaps another ten years. The last few were not described as pleasant. Radioactive poisoning would corrode her from the inside out.

Miraculously, Natalia has survived and is sharing her story with others. It is a beautiful message of making the most of the time you are given.

She shared something with me that I thought was interesting. She said that our purpose with the time we are given should be to share the gifts of our values for the benefit of others.

The viewpoint that our values are not simply internal guideposts for our decisions but are our **gifts to others** and that **those gifts are to be shared**, is a wonderful way to approach determining your next plateau. Aligning your next plateau with the purpose of sharing the gifts of your values can help you clarify your real goals and surmount the obstacles that so often prevent people from even visualizing their next plateau.

PROBING QUESTIONS

Imagine you are sitting at the black granite table in my office. We're discussing your next plateau. We talk about retirement, buying or selling a business or second home, changing jobs or careers. This massive decision faces you.

Many times, internal thoughts can quickly sabotage the exercise. It's tempting to begin to visualize the next plateau as what you think others expect it to be. But this is *your* plateau. The only things that exist there are what you imagine there to be. The decision to grow doesn't have to be the acquisition of material wealth. It doesn't have to be fancy cars and houses. Although, if that's what you're about, go for it. Presupposing that the next plateau must hold something other than what you would want is a horrible way to start.

When visualizing, don't feel constrained by social expectations, finances, or time. This part of the process is for expanding the possibilities. We will come back and make sure the visualization is realistic and affordable later. For now, look to that plateau — the one you have been avoiding. What does it look like?

If you still can't quite see it, ask yourself some clarifying questions.

What Do You Regret?

"Live with no regrets." It's probably some of the worst advice, yet everyone assumes it is correct. In his book, *The Power of Regret,* Daniel Pink explores the various types of regret and digs into how rather than avoid regret, we should embrace the feeling.[61] It can inform future behavior and decisions. If you regret losing your temper with a colleague and now use that recognition to moderate your behavior, well, that's regret working its magic to build a more positive life for you moving forward.

If we embrace regret, we learn from it and make better decisions.

One of the questions I will ask those seeking to make a Plateau Jump begins with exploring where they are now. We talk about the gratitude for what they have achieved, as we discussed earlier in this book. We talk about their successes. Perhaps it's the wealth they have achieved or the business or family they have built.

The question I'll ask, and one you should ask yourself, is, "What has all this success cost you?"

It's a tough question to ask and even more difficult to answer for some people. Not that we don't know the answer, but saying it comes with some vulnerability.

For many people, as they look back to previous plateaus, it's easy to have a sense of gratitude for what they have achieved to get to where they are now. But those previous plateaus may have come at a cost. To the extent that the cost brings regret about previous decision-making, that regret then informs the vision of your next plateau. Where you jump next and how you get there will be directed by the learnings that regret created.

Evaluate what getting to your current plateau has cost you. Maybe you set aside a music career to raise a family. Maybe you neglected family relationships or your health to build a business. Maybe you neglected friends for the sake of hobbies. What did you have to sacrifice? That can be a great place to start when beginning to envision what the next plateau should hold for you.

Are You Looking in the Right Place?

"How many of you are happy with the money you're making?"

It was the speaker's opening line for his presentation. I sat near the back of the auditorium, ready to make an early exit from the conference if this final presentation of the day wasn't anything that grabbed my attention. When I heard that comment, I started to gather my belongings. It had been a long day of meetings. Listening to yet another speaker ramble on about how to generate better business results was starting to feel repetitive.

But then I noticed a good portion of the attendees in the room had raised their hands in answer to the question. This was a group of wealthy, high-earning financial advisors. Of course, they were happy with the money they were making. I paused, knowing this was going to wreck this guy's presentation if he couldn't connect to the need for the audience to want to go to the next level and do more. Was I about to watch a presentation train wreck?

I sat my stuff back down and waited to see how the speaker was going to recover. How was his presentation going to continue if the audience did not want to "take it to the next level," as we had been hearing about all day? A quiet murmur of laughter swept over the room because everyone saw what I saw.

The presenter wasn't prepared for that response. There was an uncomfortable pause.

Then, the speaker recovered. He improvised a line that wasn't in his presentation. "I wonder, then, why it takes you all year to earn it?"

Nice save.

So many times, we fall into the trap of assuming the next plateau must be more or must be bigger. It doesn't. It should represent growth.

The next plateau may not be where you are used to looking. I started thinking about his improvised question. If most people in this room are happy with their income, why does it take all year to earn it? The next plateau could be more autonomy. The next plateau could be seeking more freedom of time. The next plateau could be fewer new clients but deeper relationships. To do any of those things, I would have to make changes in my systems, goals, habits, relationships, or, most of all, beliefs.

The following year, I committed to spending more time with the family. I scheduled more time away from the office. The second year after, I doubled that and took two consecutive months away and began taking the family places where we could do things we had never done. We started learning new skills like sailing, scuba diving, ice climbing, and paragliding. We sought new adventures together. New plateaus.

Is What You Want Aligned with Your Values and Purpose?

When I was an impressionable young boy, my grandfather was the richest man I knew. He wasn't actually what you

SO MANY TIMES,
WE FALL INTO THE
TRAP OF ASSUMING
THE NEXT PLATEAU
MUST BE MORE OR
MUST BE BIGGER.
IT DOESN'T. IT SHOULD
REPRESENT GROWTH.

would call rich, but in the eyes of a young boy, his life was wondrous. We would drive out to see him on his small farm just north of Dallas. The expansiveness of the land he owned was awe-inspiring to me at the time.

As we drove up the long gravel driveway to his farmhouse, I looked out over the fields where his cattle grazed. When we stopped, I immediately ran out of the car to go play in the barn with my sister. We would climb on the tractor, jump on the hay bales, feed the horses, and just explore the surrounding land.

Those were the kinds of things kids did before the internet. And we had the kind of awe kids have when their idea of rich is money and things.

But he was so rich that all he had was money and things. When he passed, the money and things vanished. There was no effective estate plan. The land and things were sold. The wealth was distributed and quickly spent by the heirs.

If you ask what his money is doing today, no one can tell you. It is somewhere doing something, but its purpose, never fully articulated, was never fully realized. It is no longer in the hands of anyone my grandfather knew. Imagine what could have been if he had made a Plateau Jump, and that plateau involved living out his values and passing them along to people and organizations he cared about through a clear plan that he shared with them. There is wealth beyond money and things, and the greatest tragedy is when that is squandered.

Your values and their role in your life are a type of wealth. I often ask clients a simple envisioning question when it comes to thinking about the purpose of their wealth. The question is: What do you want your wealth to do when you're done using it?

It's a simple question, but I almost never get the true answer the first time around. Often, the answer I get will be something to the tune of, "I want it to go to my kids," or to their spouse, church, charity, etc. I always point out that the answer they have given me tells me *where* they want the wealth to go but not *what* they want the wealth to do.

Imagine that your wealth has a life of its own and that that life outlives you. That money will go somewhere, and that somewhere should have a purpose.

Your next plateau needs to become the next expression of that purpose — real in thoughts, words, and actions. It needs to have a purpose that can provide a bigger future.

Is What You Want Affordable?

There is an obvious question of monetary affordability to any Plateau Jump, but for our purposes, I am going to expand on what we discussed in Chapter 7. Will you, and can you, do what it takes to get there?

To answer that question, you must know *what* it takes. First, you need to know where you are relative to the change you want to make. You must be able to visualize what the Wall of Change requires of you. Only then will you know how to answer the question of *what* it will take. Until you know what it will take, you can't answer the question of you being willing and able to expend the time, energy, and capital.

You must possess the resources of time, energy, and capital to expend them. You'll need to know how much. Can you free up the time? Do you have enough daily energy? If not, what changes in your systems or habits need to occur?

If you are committing to expending time and energy, you will need to first possess the motivation that provides the willingness. There must be a deep and clear connection to your intrinsic motivation. You may, however, not possess enough motivation. None of us do. You'll need discipline. From that discipline will grow habits. That's where the levers of Habits and Systems come in.

You'll also need the ability and competency to provide the resources. Willingness alone can't get you to the next plateau if you are unable to make the jump. I may want to play in the NFL, but if I lack physical ability (and I do), it doesn't matter how motivated I am. If you don't possess the resources currently, then those can come from making changes in your Goals and Relationships. You may be able to connect with someone who can help. (I still wouldn't make it to the NFL with that strategy, but you get the idea.)

Is What You Want Accessible?

Any plateau we seek needs to be realistic and achievable. The math should work. Obviously, you're not going to envision a new plateau of playing in the New York Philharmonic Orchestra if you only have a few minutes a day to practice.

The question of accessibility is primarily one of visualization. Can you realistically visualize the next plateau? Try writing down what you want to see happen. Writing down the details and specifics can help clarify your thoughts. You may not ever fully know what you think until you write it down. Meditate on what you want to see happen. Create a clear mental space to envision the next plateau. In the following chapter, we'll go through a Wall of Change exercise, which will help you see the details even more clearly. If you are unable to see the details of this new plateau, it may not be accessible to you quite yet.

Consider bringing in a coach to assist you or getting a mentor who has been on the next plateau already. These represent changes in relationships. You'll want a meaningful and compelling next plateau that doesn't overwhelm you. While a certain degree of risk-taking and ambition is healthy, there is no sense in setting unattainable targets. That's why breaking the jump into goals of 90-day targets is helpful.

ASK PROFOUND LIFE-PLANNING QUESTIONS

The following questions are based on the thinking of George Kinder, author of *The Seven Stages of Money Maturity: Understanding the Spirit and Value of Money in Your Life.*[62] Many advisors and life coaches will use versions of George's excellent questions in their discussions with those seeking to jump to the next plateau. These are open-ended questions to get you thinking about what you want and remove the thought barriers of the constraints we may normally apply.

The initial question I use invites you to envision a future where health and financial constraints don't exist, prompting you to consider how you would lead your life under such circumstances. What would you do with your time? How would you contribute to society?

What would you do if you were unconstrained by concerns of wealth, health, or time?

This question is the essence of mental freedom. It encourages imaginative thinking and visualization. It allows you to detach yourself from current financial, social, and time constraints and explore your deepest desires and aspirations. By envisioning a life of financial security, you are prompted to reflect on your intrinsic motivations, values, and priorities. It helps you identify what truly matters to you and how you would spend your time and contribute to society if financial worries were removed.

The second question applies constraints of time while allowing you to retain good health and all the wealth you would need. Now, you begin to think about how things would change. What would you do differently?

If you had your wealth and health but a limited amount of time left to live, how would your first answer change?

In a hypothetical scenario of limited time left to live, you are free from health and wealth constraints but are aware that your lifetime is finite. The question challenges you to contemplate the implications of mortality and consider the urgency of making the most of the time you have. What truly matters to you? What would you prioritize if you had limited time left (which, of course, you do)?

The next question amplifies the time constraint and forces you to deal with your own mortality in a more urgent way. As time grows short, it's your chance to consider those things most important to you.

If you had your wealth but now only 48 hours to live, how would you spend your final days?

Regrets are the powerful visualization tool we discussed earlier in this chapter. Why not start by visualizing the next plateau as the things you would otherwise regret not having done?

Next, we think about relationships with others.

What would you like people to say about you? How would you like to be remembered?

This question invites introspection and reflection on your personal identity and your impact on others. It invites you to consider the legacy you want to leave behind and how it can help others and the world. It asks you to project yourself into the future and imagine how you want to be remembered.

In his book *The Seven Habits of Highly Effective People*, Stephen Covey illustrates Habit #2, "Begin with the end in mind," by inviting readers to embark on an interesting exercise: crafting a vivid narrative of their own funeral and eulogy.[63] While this proposition may initially strike some as macabre, its potential impact is remarkable, serving as a powerful tool for cultivating a forward-thinking mindset.

Now, we have one more question, leading back to regret — this time, not what you've done, but what you've missed. What did you not get to do?

What have you always wanted to achieve but haven't yet done — better yet, what would you regret never having accomplished?

That final question often brings out the "hidden obstacle," the one that no one has seen yet because it's based on a regret of something that doesn't exist. It forces you to think about the things you've pushed to the back of your mind.

All of these questions engage your imagination and introspective thinking. They tap into your emotions and values, helping you uncover what truly matters to you, and can serve as catalysts for personal growth, goal-setting, and decision-making.

STEPPING INTO THE UNKNOWN WITH NEW GIFTS TO SHARE

Nancy arrived at my office a few minutes early. I could feel the energy in her voice as she chatted with my assistant in the lobby. So as not to miss the story she was sharing, I came out to meet her and saw she had brought photos. She had just come back from a short hiking trip in Yosemite and was thanking us for the travel guidebook we had sent in advance of the trip.

As we sat down at the black granite table in my office, I paused and asked, "How was it?" She knew I wasn't just asking about the hike. Harry had passed away eight months prior, and this was her first time traveling without him.

"Traveling without Harry is different," she replied. "He used to take care of the arrangements. Now it's up to me." She smiled and added, "I'm not trying to do these trips on a budget like Harry would."

Then she explained further. "For the past couple of years, I was home with Harry. I don't want to say I was stuck there because that sounds awful. I wanted to be there for him, and I'm glad I could be. But I did feel like I was on a plateau like you talk about because, in a sense, I couldn't move from there. Now that I can, I want to."

I wanted to say something but just listened instead. Nancy was describing her Plateau Jump and didn't need me getting in the way.

"There are things I still want to do," she went on. "I want to take care of my health and go do more hiking trips. I've already hired a trainer so I can get in better shape to do that." She let out an exhale and made a face that let me know that hard work had already started. "I've set my sites on a Rim-to-Rim Grand Canyon Hike next year! Then I'm doing the Narrows in Zion National Park in Utah sometime after that." This was a big deal for Nancy, who had never been a big adventurer. The Narrows is a popular hike in Zion Canyon, and I knew it was located on the Colorado Plateau. That little coincidence made me smile.

Then she began to explain a more significant Plateau Jump that lined up with what had motivated her to share her values with me years earlier. She was aligning herself with her motivation to help improve the lives of others.

She paused and said, "I also want to make a bigger impact with the foundation we set up. There are women who come to the mission where I volunteer, and they've lost their husbands like I have. Harry and I were lucky in that we had the resources to pay for the expenses when he got sick. Not everyone is so fortunate. I want to find a way to use the foundation to help women at the mission where I volunteer."

"Sounds like we have some work to do," I said, smiling.

Turning a Plateau Jump outward toward others and expressing the gift of your values toward a worthy goal? It's difficult to think of a better jump than that.

Plateau Jumps can be small, or they can be large, but they all involve change, and they all should take you to a place that compels you to action and excites you. They should all create a compelling future.

To determine if your next plateau is aligned with your bigger purpose, you need to know what that purpose is — even if it surprises you.

PLATEAU-JUMPING QUESTIONS

Is there a plateau you're seeking that involves
less of something?

What has getting to your current plateau cost you?

Can that cost inform your next plateau?

Is there a plateau you regret avoiding as you journeyed to the one you now occupy?

Is there an accessible plateau ahead you are closing your mind off to?

CHAPTER 12

Take Your Plateau Higher

REMARKABILITY JUMPS ALL

"If you're brave enough to say goodbye, life will reward you with a new hello."
— PAULO COELHO

"Life is really about moving on, owning an enthusiasm for life, getting a better perspective, having heart, and being able to elevate your spirit so that life is not daunting, it's an adventure." — BILL WALTON, NBA HALL OF FAME

SEVERAL YEARS AGO, I took the family to Boston on a short vacation. I was there to meet with an investment company as due diligence for a portfolio we were building for a client. My family came along to see the sights. We checked into the Four Seasons near the Boston Commons. When we walked into the spacious lobby after dropping off our car with the valet, something interesting happened. The person behind the counter greeted me by name, "Welcome back, Mr. Smith!"

During my time checking in with the valet up front, they had radioed ahead that I was coming in. The person behind the counter had checked their records to notice that I had stayed there before. They not only greeted me by name but made sure to say, "Welcome back." Now I was feeling special.

It got even better when we got to the rooms. We had two rooms, one for the kids and one for my wife and myself. Our room was everything we expected. It was beautifully appointed and clean, and it had everything we needed.

We went next door to the kids' room and found something remarkable. The hotel had noticed that we were checking in with our children when we made the reservation. When we got to their room next to ours, there was a special tray of treats just for them! Three little stuffed bears and cookies and milk, just for them. What do you think is our kids' favorite hotel?

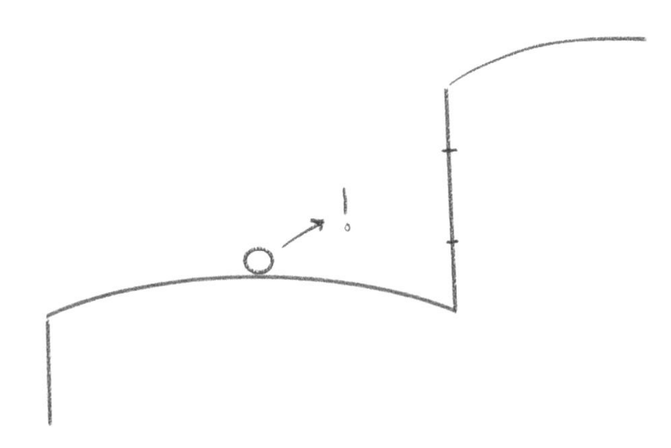

THREE POINTS OF CHANGE

There are three Points of Change that must be addressed to successfully complete the jump to the next plateau: the Point of Acceptance, the Point of Distinction, and the Point of Remarkability.

Each point is at a higher level up the Wall of Change to the next plateau. The process of mentally working through each of these points is useful in visualizing the next plateau.

Why visualize the Wall of Change at these three points?

The idea is that as you begin to visualize, your creativity begins to work on your energy. You begin by imagining what is minimally needed at the new plateau that doesn't exist at the current one. This Point of Acceptance is, in essence, the preparatory step. These are the basics that you must create. Those should come easily.

Next, you begin to enhance those basics to create distinctions, those small differences that are unique to your journey. The energy grows, and creativity blossoms.

Then, you begin to imagine those Points of Remarkability that really get you excited about the possibilities.

There is more to this than just wishing upon a star. It is a potent tool, with neuroscience suggesting that the brain often struggles to differentiate between a vividly imagined event and an actual one. Visualizing that Point of Remarkability can actually help you make the jump.

In a study from Harvard Medical School, researchers discovered that piano players who visualized playing a piece of music activated the same brain regions as those who physically played the music.[64]

Essentially, the act of visualization was creating neural patterns in the brain, mimicking the patterns created by actual practice. To our brain, those things we visualize feel just like those things we do. When we visualize an act or outcome, such as a Point of Remarkability, the neurons in our brain mirror that activity, creating a neural blueprint.

This neural mimicry has profound implications for visualizing the next plateau and jumping there. When we visualize achieving a particular goal or outcome, the brain starts developing patterns and connections as if the event has already occurred. This makes the next plateau seem more tangible and real, thus enhancing energy and motivation. The Four Seasons Boston had climbed the Wall of Change from other hotels we had stayed in. The Point of Acceptance (clean rooms) had been met. The Point of Distinction (greeting me by name) and then the Point of Remarkability (special treats for the kids) were present. It made it so easy to see how this hotel was operating at a different level from others in its industry. They could have stopped at simply providing a clean room, but they didn't.

When looking to make a Plateau Jump, it is helpful to break the jump into these three points to wrap your mind around it. Envision what occurs at the next level. You have no idea since you can't see up there, but you can imagine. What do you imagine people who exist at this new plateau do? How do they act? What competencies do they possess?

If we think about these questions in three parts, the answers become easier, and the excitement and energy grow as you imagine existing at your new level. Let's examine these points more deeply so you can see what I mean.

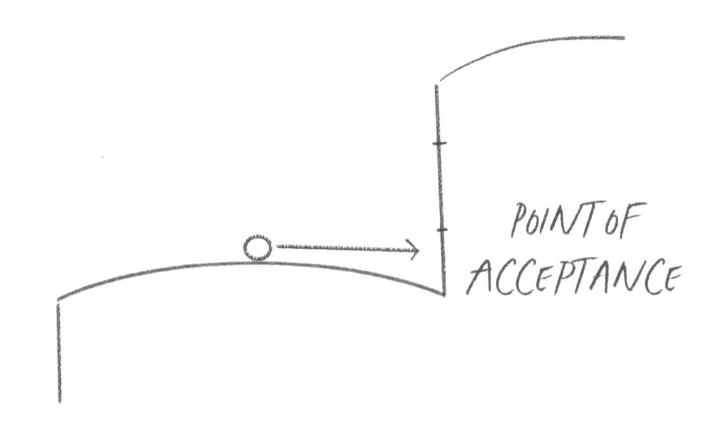

Point of Acceptance (The Ante)

First, a Point of Acceptance is the tasks and behaviors you think about automatically when you think about existence at the next plateau. When we visualize what must be minimally present at the next level of accomplishment, we set a tangible target that galvanizes our determination and perseverance. What is the expected level of behavior or competency? How does that look different from what you are doing now?

You'll often encounter barriers that impede your progress. These barriers manifest as self-doubt, fear of failure, or a lack of clarity about what lies ahead. However, at the first level of the Wall of Change, known as the Point of Acceptance, you can confront these barriers head-on. This level of visualization challenges you to anticipate and embrace what will be expected of you at the next stage of your journey.

Imagine yourself as a talented athlete aiming to reach the next level of your sport. You have excelled in your current arena, but to advance, you must face the Point of Acceptance — a plateau where new challenges await. It is here that you recognize what will be expected of you on the next plateau. The Point of Acceptance represents the minimum threshold of performance required at the next plateau; it's the ante to play there. That's a level that you expect to achieve.

What will happen at the next plateau that isn't present in your life now? For example, if that change is retirement, think past that first day of sleeping in without an alarm clock and begin to think about what really happens.

Go beyond those first few weeks or months of travel and golf. What is your purpose there at that new plateau?

Because many of the things you are leaving behind at the former plateau still need to exist at the new plateau. Social interaction, income, medical benefits. These are the basics before we move on. Where will they come from?

If you are starting a new business, what basic goods or services will you provide? If it is a new skill or adventure, then ask yourself what basic skills you'll need. These are the first and fundamental questions to start with.

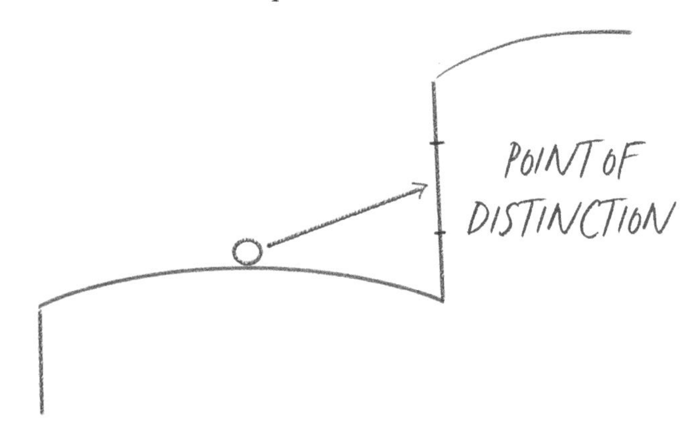

Point of Distinction (Just Noticeable Difference)

Once you've found your Point of Acceptance, it's time to aim for the Point of Distinction. But what, exactly, is the Point of Distinction? Well, think of it as that moment when your efforts become unmistakably noticeable.

Let me explain it in simple terms: Imagine you're holding a book, and someone adds a feather to it. You probably won't notice at first. But add another feather and another — there comes a point when you suddenly realize the difference. That's the Point of Distinction.

Ernst Weber and Gustav Fechner were pioneering German psychologists and experimentalists who made significant contributions to the field of psychophysics, the branch of psychology that deals with the relationship between physical stimuli and sensory perceptions.

Weber was obsessed with understanding how we perceive touch. He coined the term "Just Noticeable Difference" (JND).[65] In plain language, it's the difference threshold, or smallest change between two things, that catches the attention of at least half the people. Just like when your coffee has that tiny bit too much sugar — you can taste it.

Weber's quest was to pinpoint that line where change becomes noticeable. It's like finding the sweet spot of transformation, where your actions become substantial.

Now, Gustav Fechner, building on Weber's ideas, took it to the next level. He dug into how we humans perceive various stimuli — sounds, lights, you name it. He birthed the field of "psychophysics," which unravels how the world outside affects what stirs within us.[66]

The Point of Distinction is, in essence, that point on your journey where what you are striving for and accomplishing begins to feel different and impactful to you and to others. They're not limited to touch; they apply to all your senses and all your endeavors. When you're envisioning a change, it might seem daunting to grasp how to get there. But remember, it all begins by identifying those small, subtle points of distinction — the moments when your efforts truly count. Embrace the idea that small changes, over time, add up to something extraordinary.

To optimize various aspects of your life, start small. For example, adjust your alarm five minutes earlier for better time management; declutter a little every day rather than trying a big clear-out; increase your reading by a page nightly;

drink an additional glass of water daily. Small changes can lead to significant results.

As you envision your next plateau, you'll start with the Point of Acceptance. You'll then start adding the Points of Distinction to incrementally enhance those initial ideas for change that can help you begin to climb that Wall of Change.

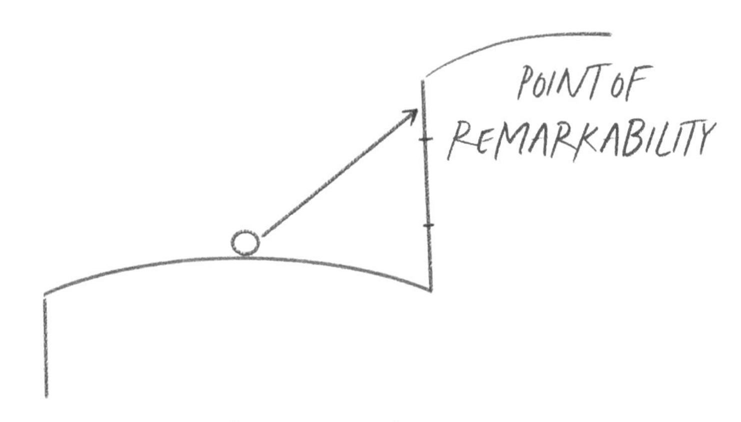

Point of Remarkability (Tell Someone)

As you envision your next plateau, now ask yourself what would make this experience truly remarkable. Notice how the energy level connects with your imagination. The pursuit of mastery has been identified as a key factor in motivation.[67] The highest level of visualization, the Point of Remarkability, connects to your intrinsic motivations, values, and purpose. When you visualize what would make the change you seek, truly remarkable things happen. You tap into the innermost desires, aligning your actions with your authentic self. You'll fuel your motivation with a deep sense of purpose.

As you ascend the Wall of Change, you reach the pinnacle: the Point of Remarkability. This phase represents the epitome of personal growth visualization. It's where you exceed expectations and become truly exceptional at your next plateau. At this level, your visualization extends beyond mere competence; it taps into your intrinsic motivations, aligns with your values, and propels you toward your ideal self.

In his book, *The 4-Hour Workweek*, Tim Ferriss suggests that reading just three books on a specific topic can make you an expert.[68] While this may hold true for basic knowledge, the Point of Remarkability demands a deeper level of mastery. Malcolm Gladwell, pulling from the work of Andres Ericsson[69], mentions the concept of the "10,000-hour rule" in his book *Outliers*[70], which emphasizes the need for extensive practice to achieve remarkable expertise and mastery.

Sure, you can do the basics of what is expected up there (the Point of Acceptance), and you can even do some unique things (Point of Distinction), but now, add the fact that there is present in you a mastery. A mastery of sharing the gifts of your values and aligned with your intrinsic motivations.

The purpose of breaking the jump into these three sections is simple. Make the Plateau Jump more manageable by compartmentalizing the changes. This makes the goal achievement easier to digest. You may notice that as you expand your thinking, the ideas that come to you at first won't necessarily be your best or most exciting. Those that come when thinking about the Point of Remarkability will no doubt be the most creative, unique, and inspiring.

Remember that all these Points of Change will need to be put through your personal acid test. They need to be things you can and will pay the price with your time and energy to accomplish. This is particularly true of the Point of

Remarkability ideas you come up with. Make sure you have the capability and motivation to accomplish them.

When you start listing the changes required to ascend to your next plateau, the changes required at the Point of Acceptance will come easily. The ideas at the Point of Distinction will come more slowly. They will challenge you.

When you visualize the Point of Remarkability, those are some of your best ideas! You may notice that as you engage in the mental exercise of listing the Points of Remarkability, your energy level increases. You're excited about the possibilities. You will become so accomplished at living your values at the new plateau that people notice. They remark on it.

How does your energy level feel? Now, jump.

Try something: Imagine you are leaving for a journey. You are released from obligations. You can stay on the journey as long as you like. Your new leather suitcases are packed; you smell the leather. You are looking sharp and feeling even better. In your checking and investment accounts exists all the money you will ever need. You step outside into a beautiful sunny day. The air smells fresh. You lock the door behind you. Glancing at your schedule, you check over the next two weeks. Now ask:

Where are you going?

What is on your schedule?

What will you learn, experience, or accomplish?

How does this align with your values and intrinsic motivations?

Who travels with you?

How did that feel? What did you start to experience? Anticipation? Fear? Excitement? Something else? Take yourself through that exercise a few times until the only result left is to jump.

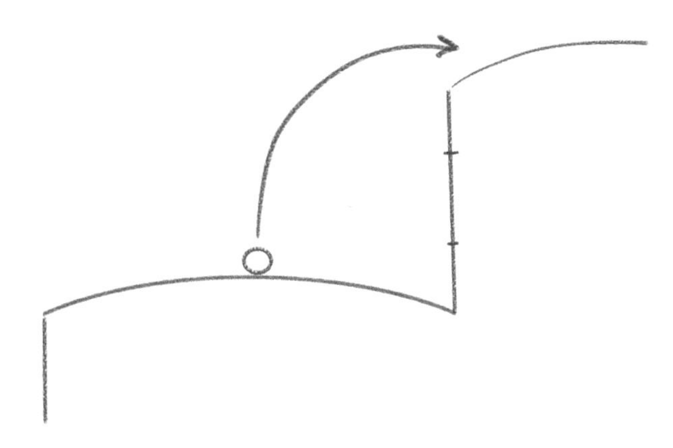

CLIMB THE WALL TO THE NEXT PLATEAU

In the picturesque region of Brixen, Italy, in the years following World War II, a young boy felt an irresistible pull toward the peaks that surrounded his home. Mesmerized by their majestic allure, he embarked on his first mountain climb at the age of five. This early encounter with the surrounding heights would spark a flame within him, igniting a lifelong obsession with mountaineering.

That boy was Reinhold Messner. Reinhold and his brother Günther soon built a bond forged out of climbing. It may have been that they climbed to escape the household of an abusive father, or it may have been the adventure. Whatever the motivation, they became without equals in the climbing community.

In 1970, as part of a large German-led team, the brothers were invited to attempt the previously unclimbed Rupal

Face of Nanga Parbat in Pakistan. The mountain stands at 26,660 feet, and the face is the largest, highest rock wall in the world — a vertical wilderness that nearly defies the laws of gravity.

Much of the time allotted for the Naga Parbat expedition had to be spent establishing increasingly higher camps where none had existed. It was slow work. As they battled the deteriorating weather, the clock was running out on their permit to stay in Pakistan. A successful summit was not looking likely.

On June 27, with only a few days left on their permit, the weather cleared, and Reinhold jumped at the brief window of opportunity. Frustrated with the delays and the expedition leadership, he started up the Rupal Face alone.[71] He found the climbing easier than what the mountaineering community had feared. But climbing alone at that elevation, if you make a mistake, no one is coming to save you.

Soon, he noticed he was not alone. Günther had left the camp as well and was hurrying to catch him. He did, and the brothers were able to summit together just before sunset. Too late to start a descent, they remained on the mountain. They were stuck there for the night without the proper gear to protect them from the bitter cold. It was a long, miserable night.

Two days later, Reinhold showed up in the valley on the other side of the mountain. He was hallucinating and had lost several toes to frostbite, but he had made it back.[72]

But just as he had started his ascent alone, he would finish alone. Fate dealt a cruel blow. Günther fell during the descent. His loss amidst the unforgiving terrain forever etched a sorrowful chapter in Reinhold's life.

Undeterred by the tragedy, Messner sought solace in the challenge of Mount Everest. He teamed up with Peter Habeler in 1978 for a daring attempt: to be the first to conquer Everest without the aid of supplemental oxygen — a feat thought impossible.

Every step became a testament to human endurance as the duo ascended into the death zone, where oxygen is so limited you are slowly dying as you climb. As the summit got closer, their triumphant ascent became an indelible mark on the annals of mountaineering history. Success came in May of that year as they became the first team to do the "impossible."

Immediately, Messner moved to another Point of Remarkability, a multi-peak climbing feat known as the "Crown of the Himalaya." Messner would summit all 14 of the world's peaks over 8,000 meters without supplemental oxygen, pushing the limits of human potential. Messner's true summit of Mount Annapurna was challenged by a few feet in late September of 2023, but this is akin to claiming Michael Jordan isn't the greatest because he committed a foul one time that wasn't caught by the refs. It misses the point.

In the early stages of his quest, Messner faced psychological barriers that threatened to derail his dreams. The lure of the familiar, the fear of the unknown, and the psychological scars of past failures posed significant challenges. These mental hurdles are what get us stuck, preventing us from venturing into uncharted territories and hindering our ability to climb our own Wall of Change.

It's quite possible to transcend the intractable inertia that holds us in place. Intractable inertia is the stubborn resistance to change and the tendency to remain stuck in our current state despite knowing that growth and progress are possible.

Here are some tips to embark on your own ascent of the Wall of Change:

1. **Visualize the goal:** Imagine the goal in the three levels we discussed. Notice that when you start imagining the third, the Point of Remarkability, the ideas will start to flow.

2. **Seek support as you plan:** Surround yourself with a supportive network of individuals who believe in your potential and have been there before, or at least (as in Messner's case) can help map out a compelling path to the unknown.

3. **Embrace discomfort as you jump:** Recognize that change often necessitates discomfort and uncertainty. Embrace the challenges as opportunities for growth, knowing that your objective lies just beyond the familiar. I heard a hiking guide perfectly explain it as "embracing the suck." Using your next plateau as a guide, control the direction and change course as needed.

By understanding the physical and mental battles Reinhold Messner faced, we can draw parallels to our own lives and find inspiration to break free from the current plateau. You have your own Point of Remarkability to ascend to. Once you have achieved that level, from there is where you will see all the other mountains you can climb that you never could see before.

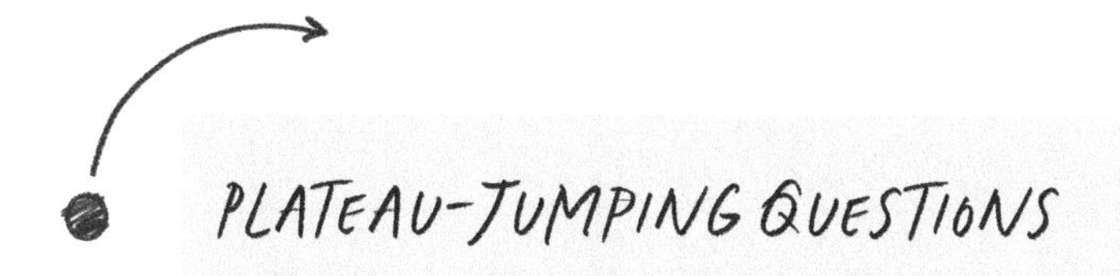

PLATEAU-JUMPING QUESTIONS

POINT OF ACCEPTANCE: Reflecting on this next plateau, what are the natural expectations or the "ante" required of you once you reach it?

What happens at the next plateau for you that isn't happening now?

POINT OF DISTINCTION: What enhancements to your Point of Acceptance can you make that would be noticeable by at least 50 percent of those who observe it?

POINT OF REMARKABILITY: What actions can you take to consistently exceed expectations and go above and beyond what is normally required or anticipated?

What aspect of existing at the next plateau gets you most energized?

CHAPTER 13

Face Your Fear

DECISION TRUMPS INACTION

"Take the first step in faith. You don't have to see the whole staircase, just take the first step." — MARTIN LUTHER KING JR.

"In any given moment, we have two options: to step forward into growth or to step back into safety." — ABRAHAM MASLOW, PSYCHOLOGIST

SEVERAL YEARS AGO, my wife Melissa and I took an early-morning hot-air balloon ride. The ride was a gift from a wealthy friend, bought as a thank-you for some planning work I had done for a beautiful chapel that would bear her name.

We had watched the same hot-air balloon take off a few weeks prior as we stood in that very spot, looking down onto the field below us one cool pre-dawn morning during a concrete pour. In the field below, they prepared the balloon and gently took off as we gazed, unable to take our eyes off the glowing sight.

"Wouldn't that be awesome to do?" I quietly mentioned, half to myself. My friend silently took mental note of my comment, tracked down the owner of the balloon, and paid him to take my wife and me up on the next calm morning.

So, several weeks later, one October morning, as the sun was just coming up and the frost still formed on our breath, we gathered again at that very job site. Under the newly visible outline of the chapel construction above us at the top of the hill, we inflated the balloon. The loud propane burner lit up the balloon and broke the silence of the morning with its intense flame. Then, in a firm and urgent voice, our pilot shouted, "GET IN!"

We scrambled up into the wicker basket. I almost didn't make it inside the basket in time for liftoff. Climbing in as it started floating away, I breathed a sigh of relief.

We took off, drifting across parts of town we had lived in most of our lives. We floated over Texas Christian University, where we had first met. We pointed out the football stadium, the restaurants, and the classroom buildings. We recognized houses of friends. It was all there. Now, we could see things from a different perspective. The landscape would look unfamiliar, and then suddenly, it would snap into recognition.

Once you look at something from a different perspective, it is difficult to see it the same way. The landscape hadn't changed. My perception had changed. As a result, I was unable to recognize some obvious sites right away. At the same time, I noticed landmarks that had always been there, yet I had been oblivious to them from my landbound point of view.

We floated to the outskirts of town. I began to wonder how a hot air balloon landed. Would we be just touching down in a field of daisies soft as a kitten's kiss? No.

Our pilot turned to us and said, "Ok, here is how it's going to go. We are going to hit over there."

Did he just say "hit"?

"When we hit," he continued, "we are going to pitch sideways about forty-five degrees." Then he looked us in the eyes. "Don't jump out! If either of you jumps out, the rest of us are going back up! So, hold on!"

He was right — we hit and pitched sideways, then righted ourselves and stopped. I wasn't letting go until he said we could, so I froze, gripping the sides of the basket. And then we were on the ground.

"Ok! We made it!"

PERCEPTION IS REALITY

Perspectives usually don't change easily. Most people have to hit something to jar them into taking a new point of view. A bankruptcy, divorce, jail, business partnership dissolution, getting fired — those are big hits. They happen at the immovable Canyon Wall.

If you look closely from the Campground, the high point, you can see yourself approaching the Canyon Wall. It happens slowly, then all at once. You don't recognize that it's happening, and then, all of a sudden, you do. You can shift that perspective before the jarring hit that will eventually come happens. When you see it clearly, it fuels your motivation to change.

Our perspective is the lens through which we see things. For Melissa and me, all the landmarks we flew over were always there, but now, we had seen them in a new way. Plateaus are no different. Our perspectives of where we are standing impact our attitudes. These perspectives impact how we move through the plateau phases and whether we jump or feel stuck.

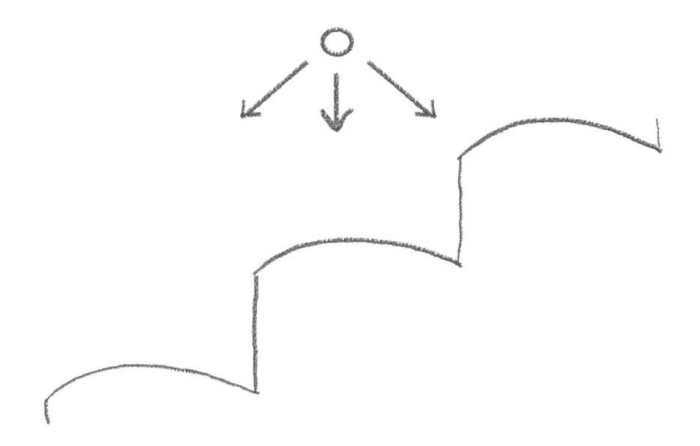

These perspectives will impact our motivations as well. Our perspectives can disorient our motivations. They can supplant internal motivations like personal growth or goals, replacing them with external motivations like praise, awards, or other tangible rewards. Our perspective must be clear and aligned with our intrinsic motivations and values.

When looking at the next plateau, we can never be certain of what we are seeing if the lens we are viewing it through is smudged. If we are not careful, fear can smudge our lens, making us hesitate to jump.

Indecisiveness can trap you in a state of analysis paralysis, where you overthink and overanalyze options to the point of becoming immobilized. This can hinder your ability to move forward and achieve your goals. But it's typical. Most people don't want to change until the temperature is turned up on them. They don't want to change until the pain is enough to force the issue or they have gathered all the facts to eliminate the risks. Most people won't jump unless the vision of the next plateau is bigger than their fears.

MOST PEOPLE WON'T JUMP UNLESS THE VISION OF THE NEXT PLATEAU IS BIGGER THAN THEIR FEARS.

What I have learned by co-hosting the *Decidedly* podcast with Sanger is that decision-making is at the core of our ability to jump to the next plateau. I have found that the most successful individuals are the best decision-makers. So, if you're still having trouble making this next decision, let's get to the bottom of why.

LET'S REVIEW... WHAT'S HOLDING YOU BACK?

We've done a lot of work through this book, with each exercise and thought process designed to take you one step further toward jumping. If you've made it to this point and you're still feeling fear, we need to review everything we've done to ensure we haven't missed anything.

1. **Determine where you're starting.** We know you're on a plateau. But is it one of your choosing, or did you fall here? Once you recognize or acknowledge the plateau you are on, begin to determine where you are on that plateau. Determine what phase you are in.

   Are you at the Cliffside, the Campground, or the Canyon Wall? Ask yourself what you need to do to get to a place of optimal energy so you can make a change of your choosing to take you where you want to go that aligns with your purpose. If you're not at the Campground, getting to that place of stability is your next step.

2. **Align your values.** Go through the process described earlier in this book so you can understand your values.

They inform your decisions, whether you acknowledge that fact or not. Your values come through in the decisions you make or don't make. They influence what you do. If you know them and can reference them, then you have a greater chance of making decisions that align with them, which is absolutely what you want. Otherwise, when you are in a state of higher emotion (when decision-making ability is at its low points), you are at the mercy of those temporal emotions. That's not a good Plateau-Jumping strategy.

3. **Know where you're jumping.** Remember, you can't simply leave a plateau; you must jump to another. That new plateau should be clearly visualized and in alignment with your own motivations and values, and as discussed, it must be affordable and accessible.

4. **Know why you're jumping.** You have to know what Simon Sinek, in his book *Start with Why*, calls your Why.[73] It is the purpose or intrinsic motivation that drives you to jump to the next plateau. Once it is clear, you can inspire others and build meaningful connections. When your Why is clear and compelling, it becomes the foundation for everything you do, guiding your decisions and actions. It helps you stay focused, motivated, and resilient in the face of challenges or setbacks.

5. **Know how you're jumping.** You need to know how you will progress to the next plateau. What elements will take you there? What levers will you pull to make the jump? You now have the Five Levers:

- Streamlined systems
- Productive habits
- Short-term compelling goals
- Meaningful relationships
- Clear beliefs

6. **Clarify the answers to your profound life questions.** This is the more detailed description of your Why — what does it look like in action? Is your motivation to express the gifts of your values? Is it to help others recognize how to reach a higher level of significance? Is it to put your wealth to its greatest and highest purpose? Perhaps something else?

7. **Determine your Point of Remarkability.** You may not achieve it immediately, but when you know what it will look like, you will have a better chance of achieving it. Not only that, the idea of that achievement and the results it will bring for others can motivate you and help tamp down your fear.

FEAR IS ALSO ENERGY

The common sentiment of being stuck or plateaued is often just a disguise for frustration, which stems from underlying fears. These fears could be of regression or negative outcomes, but the crucial shift lies in recognizing that these feelings on the plateau can be harnessed as sources of energy.

Fear's pervasive influence holds us back from reaching our potential and confines us to our comfort zones. The fear of failure, with its paralyzing grip, makes us wary of risks, but reframing it as a stepping-stone for growth and learning can liberate us.

Conversely, the fear of success can also hinder progress, but viewing it as an avenue to build and expand upon current accomplishments opens doors to new possibilities.

Fear of change, while rooted in our primal desire for safety, must be transformed into an appreciation for growth and new experiences, achieved through gradual steps.

Lastly, the fear of judgment, which often dictates decisions, can be shed by prioritizing personal goals and values, allowing for authentic living devoid of societal pressures.

Thus, embracing fear and turning it into motivation can help the jump.

DECIDE TO DECIDE

Let's face it: When it comes to deciding to make a Plateau Jump, there are only three scenarios:

You decide to jump.

You decide <u>not</u> to jump.

You fail to decide.

The only unacceptable scenario is to fail to decide. By failing to decide, you relegate your fate to the destructive effects of entropy.

It seems like an easy choice to just wait, but that's a scenario in which you don't have to justify your decision. You're just waiting for all the facts to come in, right? The problem is you may never have enough facts to decide. Sometimes, you can't know what you're missing from the hot-air balloon perspective until you actually go up in the balloon. If your fear is preventing you from taking the steps to gather new facts, it will never allow you to move.

Indecision often leads to increased stress and anxiety as you grapple with uncertainty and the fear of making the wrong choice. The constant mental turmoil of weighing options without acting will take a toll.

If you are at a point of indecision, do this: Make the decision to decide. Set a timeframe. Decide what data needs to be known to make the decision. If there is a knowable piece of data you need, make the decision to decide when the data arrives.

If the piece of data you need to make the decision is unknowable, you have to use what facts you do know and then follow your values and instincts. Your instincts can be your superpower. They are your strength. They will guide you to pull the right levers.

Recognize what you want to see happen. Of course, none of this works until you do, and nothing changes until you decide. Deciding to decide can be empowering.

In whatever way you can, even if it seems small at first...
Jump.

NONE OF THIS
WORKS UNTIL
YOU DO,
AND NOTHING
CHANGES UNTIL
YOU DECIDE.

Where are you on your current plateau?

Why are you seeking change?

How will you make it happen? What is your first step?

What is the next decision you need to make?

EPILOGUE

Another Trail, Another Lesson

UP AHEAD, THE paths diverged. I was two weeks into my month-long journey walking the Camino de Santiago, and my trail sense was getting better — but not good enough.

As I approached a turn in the trail, there sat a small, handmade sign leaning against a tree, pointing to my right. Conversely, I also noticed some sticks in the shape of a large arrow on the path at my feet, pointing to the left. There were no official Camino markings or signs to be found. I couldn't locate this turn on a map. The familiar bright yellow image of a scallop shell that had led my way up to this point was absent. I was directionless.

I made a decision and walked left. This was a fifty-fifty chance of staying on the correct path, but I was generally heading in the right direction and not too worried... at least for now.

Within a couple of miles or so, I sensed something was off. I noticed a road in the valley below me that wasn't on my map. I hadn't seen any of the landmarks mentioned in my guidebook. I was lost, moving along in the wrong direction.

The day was getting late, and backtracking to the makeshift sign against the tree at this point would mean adding miles to the already long day. Frustration was setting in. It was the frustration you get when you know you've taken yourself to a place you didn't want to go.

Up ahead, I noticed an older man walking the lonely path in my direction. He greeted me as I approached, saying, "Buen Camino." This was a typical greeting to Camino pilgrims walking the Way of Saint James, the Camino de Santiago. I returned the greeting with a pleasant "*Gracias*," being sure to say it in the Castilian dialect and not the Mexican Spanish I knew from my home in Texas. "*¿Habla inglés?*" I asked, hoping that he spoke some English.

"No," came the one-word reply as he shook his head.

"*¿Ah, dónde está el Camino?*" ("Where is the Camino?") I stumbled out, using nearly all the Spanish I knew, to ask where in the world I was and how to get to the actual trail. Quickly, I pulled out my guidebook and found the town I was trying to get to. It was the next town on the Camino. "*¿Aquí?*" pointing to the name of the town in my guidebook and asking if we were there.

The man shook his head and indicated with a wave of his finger that I was off track. I knew that already. Then he did something unexpected. He patted his chest and indicated that he wanted me to follow him.

This man knew no English but sensed correctly that I was not where I wanted to be. Now, he was offering to help.

I had exhausted what little Spanish I knew, and so we walked in silence. We walked for about an hour — three miles. Up ahead, a small village came into view. As we approached it, the man, silent for the past hour, began to speak. "*Aquí está el Camino.*" I understood enough to know what he was saying, "Here is the Camino."

As he stopped, he pointed up to the corner of the first tile-roofed stone structure we came to in the village. On the corner of the old building, there was the familiar, bright yellow scallop shell painted to indicate the way forward. Getting to the next yellow scallop shell sign was like the small goals we set to indicate directionality. The familiar yellow scallop indicated I was back on track, headed in the right direction.

My purpose wasn't simply to reach the next yellow-scallop benchmark along the trail. My purpose was to become someone who had traveled the journey of the Camino. My purpose was to be transformed by the experience. The yellow scallop shells were simply an indication I was on the right journey. Now, here it was in front of me.

For me, this journey was a Plateau Jump. I wasn't just hiking five hundred miles. I was becoming someone who experienced the journey. That experience included getting lost and finding a solution. It included self-discovery. It included learning about goals, systems, habits, relationships, and my own beliefs.

I had to change a relationship to get back on track — a relationship with myself. I did something I rarely did at home; I admitted I was lost. I stopped relying on myself and opened up to accepting help. I had sought it out. I needed a guide, and one arrived. I followed. The competitors I imagined I saw in other pilgrims on the Camino de Santiago faded away, and I began to view them as traveling their own journey on the same trail as I for a time.

I had foolishly stopped following a system of checking my map at all crossroads, and it had cost me. I had neglected the habit of checking my progress regularly, and it had gotten me lost. Again.

The man who helped me was briefly my guide in the Plateau Jump. He put me back on track. Pointing me in the right direction. I did learn that his name was Santiago. *Fitting*, I thought.

Grabbing into my pack for my phone, I wanted to snap a photo, but Santiago had already turned to make the three-mile walk back to where we had first met. From there, he would go on to wherever his own journey took him.

I held my phone with the camera app still open, then smiled as I remembered something I had once heard about the journey through life we all take. Focus on the good times, develop from the negatives, and if things don't work out, just take another shot.

Let's take another shot at staying on track, I thought.

Plateau Jumping is a lot like the Camino de Santiago or any transformative experience. You probably don't know the language; you've never been there before, and your journey will fill you with excitement and, at times, uncertainty. There will be times when you feel lost and times when you really are. If you search, you'll find the right guide.

Once you're clear about where you want to go and what sent you on the journey, you'll instinctively know what levers to pull to get to where you've envisioned.

And then you just... jump.

END NOTES

1 V. J. Shute, M. Ventura, Y.J. Kim, & D. Zapata-Rivera, "The power of plateauing: When learners achieve more by doing less," *Educational Psychologist*, Vol. 54, no. 3 (2019): 177–192.

2 T.J.M. Schopf, *Models in Paleobiology*, section by Niles Eldredge and Stephen Jay Gould, "Punctuated equilibria: An alternative to phyletic gradualism," (Freeman Cooper and Co., 1972), pp. 82-115.

3 R.L. Kahn, D.M. Wolfe, R.P. Quinn, J.D. Snoek, & R.A Rosenthal, *Organizational Stress: Studies in Role Conflict and Ambiguity* (John Wiley & Sons, 1964).

4 *Encyclopaedia Britannica,* s.v., "Plateau of Tibet," accessed October 17, 2023, https://www.britannica.com/place/Plateau-of-Tibet.

5 Bruce Feiler, *Life Is in the Transitions: Mastering Change at Any Age,* (Penguin Press: July 14, 2020).

6 Information taken from "Syd's Life," https://www.sydbarrett.com/syds-life/.

7 The Pink Floyd, "See Emily Play," June 16, 1967 (B side to "The Scarecrow").

8 Tim Ott, "Syd Barrett: How LSD Created and Destroyed His Career with Pink Floyd," Biography.com, September 8, 2020, https://www.biography.com/musicians/syd-barrett-pink-floyd.

9 Julian Palacios, *Syd Barrett, and Pink Floyd: Dark Globe* (London: Plexus Publishing Limited, 2010).
10 David Gilmour, Roger Waters, and Richard Wright, "Part I," from *Wish You Were Here,* vinyl (Harvest (UK), Columbia/CBS (US), Pink Floyd Music Publishers Ltd, September 15, 1975).
11 Ingsoc.com, "A Rambling Conversation with Roger Waters Concerning All This and That," archived from the original on November 4, 2016; retrieved July 27, 2016.
12 James O. Prochaska, and John C. Norcross, *Systems of Psychotherapy: A Transtheoretical Analysis* (New York: Oxford University Press, 2018).
13 Clarisse Dibao-Dina, Denis Angoulvant, Jean-Pierre Lebeau, Jean-Eudes Peurois, Karim Abdallah El Hirtsi, and Anne-Marie Lehr-Drylewicz, "Patients' adherence to optimal therapeutic, lifestyle and risk factors recommendations after myocardial infarction: Six years follow-up in primary care," *PLoS One* 13 no. 9 (Sep 4, 2018), doi: 10.1371/journal.pone.0202986.
14 John Miller, "Potato mogul J.R. Simplot dead at 99," *Moscow-Pullman Daily News,* May 26, 2008.
15 Richard Brandt, "J.R. Simplot: Still Hustling, after all these years," *Business Week,* September 3, 1990.
16 *The New York Times,* "Idaho's. Potato King Charged in 8 Cases of U.S. Tax Fraud," May 5, 1977.
17 Marty Trillhaase, "Simplot," *Lewiston Morning Tribune,* July 1, 1990, p. 1A.
18 H.A McGregor & A.J. Elliot, "The social nature of achievement motivation: implications for achievement motivation in social contexts," *Advances in Motivation and Achievement* 14 (2005): 113-148.

19 Conservative estimate. Actual numbers were much higher.
20 Aron Ralston, *Between a Rock and a Hard Place* (New York: Atria Books, 2004).
21 *Decidedly* podcast, Episode #54, "Dandapani: Deciding to Have Unwavering Focus: Insights from a Former Monk," September 14, 2022.
22 Dandapani, *The Power of Unwavering Focus: Focus Your Mind, Find Joy, and Manifest Your Goals* (London: Transworld Digital, 2022).
23 *Decidedly* podcast, Episode #56, "Jeremy Poincenot: Deciding to Be a Blind Golfer: On Par with Resilience and Focus," September 22, 2022.
24 Hans Selye, *The Stress of Life* (New York: McGraw-Hill, 1956). Discussed in Jackson, Mark (2012). "The pursuit of happiness," *History of the Human Sciences* 25 no. 5 (December 2012): 13–29.
25 A.J. Crum, P. Salovey, and S. Achor, "Rethinking stress: The role of mindset in determining the stress response," *Journal of personality and social psychology* 104 no. 4 (2013):716–733.
26 A. Mariotti, "The effects of chronic stress on health: new insights into the molecular mechanisms of brain-body communication," *Future Sci OA* 1 no. 3 (November 1, 2015), doi: 10.4155/fso.15.21.
27 Abigail Alling, Mark Nelson, and Sally Silverstone, *Life Under Glass: Crucial Lessons in Planetary Stewardship from Two Years in Biosphere 2* (Santa Fe, NM: Synergetic Press, November 2020).
28 L. Rochette, G. Dogon, and C. Vergely, "Stress: Eight Decades after Its Definition by Hans Selye," *Brain*

Science, 13 no. 2 (Feb 12, 2023):310. doi: 10.3390/brainsci13020310.

29 J.M. Wolf, S.R. Riedijk, A.J. Wijkhuijs, J.M. Hoogendam, G. van der Pompe, and E.C. de Lange, "Stress and cortisol responses in healthy residents exposed to short-term isolation and confinement," *Psychoneuroendocrinology* 69 (2016):17–23.

30 Daniel H. Pink, Drive: *The Surprising Truth About What Motivates Us,* (New York: Riverhead, 2011).

31 A. Fishbach, and R. Dhar, "Goals as excuses or guides: The liberating effect of perceived goal progress on choice," *Journal of Consumer Research* 32 no. 3 (2005): 370–377.

32 Fishbach, A., & Dhar, R. (2007). "When thinking beats doing: The role of optimistic expectations in goal-based choice." *Journal of Consumer Research,* 34(5), 567-578.

33 R.A. Emmons, and M.E. McCullough, "Counting blessings versus burdens: An experimental investigation of gratitude and subjective well-being in daily life," *Journal of Personality and Social Psychology* 84 no. 2 (2003): 377–389.

34 V. Peltokorpi, P. Parvinen, and M. Ruokolainen, "Work engagement and job satisfaction among those experiencing a plateau in their work tasks," *Journal of Applied Psychology* 105 no. 7 (2020): 763–773.

35 George Vaillant, *Adaptation to Life* (Harvard Press, 1977).

36 Kennon M. Sheldon and Andrew J. Elliot, "Goal Striving, Need Satisfaction, and Longitudinal Well-Being: The Self-Concordance Model," *Journal of Personality and Social Psychology* 76, no. 3 (1999): 482–497.

37 Thomas Jefferson, et al, July 4, "Copy of Declaration of Independence," July 4, 1776.

38 A.R. Todd, and T.B. Kashdan, "Volitional personality trait change: Can people choose to change their personality traits?" *Journal of Personality and Social Psychology* 96 no. 2 (2009): 490–504.

39 George T. Ainsworth-Land and Beth Jarman, *Breakpoint and Beyond: Mastering the Future Today* (Champaign, Ill.: HarperBusiness, 1992).

40 Walter Mischel and Ebbe B. Ebbesen, "Attention in delay of gratification," *Journal of Personality and Social Psychology* 16 no. 2 (1970): 329–337.

41 *City Slickers,* directed by Ron Underwood, (1991; Castle Rock Entertainment).

42 Charles Duhigg, *The Power of Habit* (London, England: Random House Books, 2013), chapter four.

43 *Decidedly* podcast, Episode #48, "Prof. Wendy Wood: Deciding to Change Your Habits: From Identification to Implementation," August 3, 2022.

44 Insurance Information Institute, auto facts + statistics alcohol impaired driving, total traffic and alcohol-impaired crash fatalities, 1985–2021, search performed November 13, 2021, iii.org.

45 Insurance Information Institute, same search, iii.org.

46 *The Graduate,* Mike Nichols, director (Embassy Pictures, 1967).

47 Centers for Disease Control and Prevention, 2019.

48 James Clear, *Atomic Habits: An Easy & Proven Way to Build Good Habits & Break Bad Ones* (Avery, 2018).

49 S.J. Scott, *Habit Stacking: 127 Small Changes to Improve Your Health, Wealth, and Happiness* (CreateSpace Independent Publishing Platform, 2014).

50 *Decidedly* podcast, Episode #17, "Doug Lennick: Deciding to Think About What You Think About," December 29, 2021.

51 *Decidedly* podcast, Episode #8, "Eric Maddox: Deciding to Find Saddam Hussein: An empathy-based approach to interrogation," October 27, 2021.

52 Ellen Langer, "Mind-Set Matters: Exercise and the Placebo Effect." *Psychological Science* 18, (2007): 165–71.

53 Marshall Goldsmith and Mark Reiter, *What Got You Here Won't Get You There: How Successful People Become Even More Successful* (New York: Hyperion, 2007).

54 Kolbe Corp., https://www.kolbe.com/.

55 *Decidedly* podcast, Episode #68, "Amy Bruske: Deciding with Your Strengths: A Flourishing Business Acumen," December 21, 2022.

56 Dominican University of California, "The Impact of Commitment, Accountability, and Written Goals on Goal Achievement," 2007.

57 S.R. Adams, N.C. Goler, R.S. Sanna, M. Boccio, D.J. Bellamy, S.D. Brown, R.S. Neugebauer, A. Ferrara, D.M. Wiley, and J.A. Schmittdiel, "Patient satisfaction and perceived success with a telephonic health coaching program: the Natural Experiments for Translation in Diabetes (NEXT-D) Study, northern California 2011," *Prev Chronic Dis.* 10 (2013).

58 James O. Prochaska, John Norcross, and Carlo DiClemente, *Changing for Good: A Revolutionary Six-Step Program for Overcoming Bad Habits and Moving Your Life Positively Forward* (Harper Collins, 1994).

59 You can find and take the Kolbe ATM Index at Kolbe.com. There is a small fee, and it will only take about 15 minutes to complete.

60 *Decidedly* podcast, Episode #34, "Natalia Matveeva: Deciding to Return to Chernobyl: A Survivor's Values-Based Journey," April 27, 2022.
61 Daniel H. Pink, *The Power of Regret: How Looking Backward Moves Us Forward* (Penguin Publishing Group, 2022).
62 George Kinder, *The Seven Stages of Money Maturity: Understanding the Spirit and Value of Money in Your Life* (Dell, 2000).
63 Stephen R. Covey, *The 7 Habits of Highly Effective People: Powerful Lessons in Personal Change* (Free Press, 1989).
64 Nicolò F. Bernardi, Matteo De Buglio, Pietro D. Trimarchi, Alfonso Chielli, and Emanuela Bricolo, "Mental practice promotes motor anticipation: evidence from skilled music performance," *Frontiers in Human Neuroscience* 7 (August 20, 2013): 451.
65 R. Biswas-Diener and E. Diener (editors), "Sensation and perception," *Noba Textbook Series: Psychology* (DEF Publishers).
66 Gustav Theodor Fechpactfulner, *Elemente der Psychophysik.* (Leipzig: Breitkopf & Härtel, 1860).
67 R.M. Ryan and E.L. Deci, *Self-determination Theory: Basic Psychological Needs in Motivation, Development, and Wellness* (Guilford Press, 2017).
68 Timothy Ferriss, *The 4-Hour Workweek: Escape 9-5, Live Anywhere, and Join the New Rich* (Crown Publishers, 2007).
69 K. Ericsson, Ralf T. Anders, Ralf, T. Krampe, and Clemens Tesch-Römer, "The Role of Deliberate Practice in the Acquisition of Expert Performance." *Psychological Review* 100, no. 3 (1993): 363–406.
70 Malcolm Gladwell, *Outliers: The Story of Success* (Little, Brown and Company, 2008).

71 Ed Caesar, "Reinhold Messner: the man who left his life on the mountain." GQ, August 30, 2020.

72 Reinhold Messner, *The Naked Mountain* (Mountaineers Books, 2003).

73 Simon Sinek, *Start with Why: How Great Leaders Inspire Everyone to Take Action* (Portfolio, 2009).

APPENDIX

Values

- Achievement
- Altruism
- Autonomy
- Belongingness
- Challenge
- Charity
- Competence
- Connection
- Control
- Courage
- Creativity
- Curiosity
- Discipline
- Empathy
- Empowerment
- Enjoyment
- Faith
- Family
- Freedom
- Friendship
- Health
- Helping others
- Humility
- Inner peace
- Innovation
- Integrity
- Joy
- Learning
- Love
- Mastery
- Meaning
- Optimism
- Open-mindedness
- Personal growth
- Philanthropy
- Purpose
- Recognition
- Religion
- Relatedness
- Responsibility

ACKNOWLEDGEMENTS

THANK YOU TO all the guests who have appeared on the *Decidedly* podcast and provided insight and wisdom in decision-making and in facing and leading change. Especially Amy Bruske, Dandapani, David Daniels, Kathy Kolbe, Doug Lennick, Eric Maddox, Jeremy Poincenot, Natalia Matveeva, and Wendy Wood, all of whose stories and wisdom became a part of this project.

Thank you to Jason Fisk, my business partner for decades, who traveled many plateaus with me and helped make the jumps possible. And, to Diane Hughes, without whom nothing gets done.

Morgan McKittrick, our esteemed producer at *Decidedly* podcast, makes our show so much fun and helps connect us with our outstanding guests.

Finally, thank you to my clients over the years who have honored me with their trust by allowing me to play a part in their Plateau Jumps, both great and small. I am proud to have been a part of our journey.

ABOUT SHAWN D. SMITH

A GRADUATE OF Texas A&M University and Texas Christian University, Shawn Smith holds designations including CFP, ChFC, and Accredited Portfolio Management Advisor. His commitment to holistic wealth management shines through his Certified Kingdom Advisor affiliation.

Delving into behavioral financial advice, Shawn navigates the intricate connection between psychology and financial choices. This unique insight helps him guide individuals toward their goals while acknowledging their emotional landscapes.

Shawn's love for hiking spans decades, and he feels the trails mirror life's lessons. Each ascent and descent unveils parallels between the challenges faced and the personal growth achieved.

In 1989, Shawn founded his financial planning practice and has been recognized by publications like *Financial Times*, *Barron's*, *Forbes*, and *Texas Monthly.*

Today, Shawn empowers entrepreneurs as a business coach and co-hosts the *Decidedly* podcast with his son Sanger. Shawn's passion is merging decision-making strategies with trail lessons, offering a transformative journey through change.

Contact Shawn

Email: shawn@decidedlypodcast.com